CHANGE
MADE EASY

I0089194

GLOBAL
PUBLISHING
G R O U P

Global Publishing Group
Australia • New Zealand • Singapore • America • London

CHANGE MADE EASY

A Simple 3 Step Process to Help You Make Effective and Lasting Change

KAREN WILSON

DISCLAIMER

All the information, techniques, skills and concepts contained within this publication are of the nature of general comment only and are not in any way recommended as individual advice. The intent is to offer a variety of information to provide a wider range of choices now and in the future, recognising that we all have widely diverse circumstances and viewpoints. Should any reader choose to make use of the information contained herein, this is their decision, and the contributors (and their companies), authors and publishers do not assume any responsibilities whatsoever under any condition or circumstances. It is recommended that the reader obtain their own independent advice.

A catalogue record for this book is available from the National Library of Australia

Published by Global Publishing Group
PO Box 517 Mt Evelyn, Victoria 3796 Australia
Email info@GlobalPublishingGroup.com.au

For further information about orders:
Phone: +61 3 9739 4686 or Fax +61 3 8648 6871

*I dedicate this book to my Mother
– a woman whose amazing generosity and capacity to love
was matched in equal measure
with a strong will and determination that could almost
drive you crazy.*

*Thanks Mum – for all of it.
Luv ya!*

BONUS OFFER

FREE for you!

As a special bonus for my readers I have created a companion workbook for the Change Made Easy process.

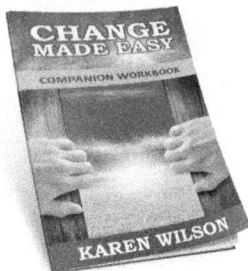

Please accept this as my gift to you.

Use it on your adventure as you explore and discover how to make change easy and create a life that you love.

DOWNLOAD YOUR FREE COPY NOW!

Go to

www.ChangeMadeEasyBook.com

Acknowledgements

This book has been a labour of love and there are a number of very special people who have contributed to making it happen. I would like to take this opportunity to say "THANK YOU" to those who have inspired, supported and encouraged me along the way. So many mentors, guides, models, colleagues and friends have influenced me and assisted in the creation of the book you now hold.

The pioneering work of Dr Bruce Lipton, Dr Joe Dispenza, Greg Brayden and Dr Masaru Emoto has broadened my mind.

Dr Wayne Dyer, Eckhart Tolle, the Dalai Lama, Gary Zukav, Louise Hay, Dan Millman and Marianne Williamson have all nourished my soul.

Sonia Choquette, John Edward, Jason McDonald, Sheila Morgan and Doreen Virtue have encouraged my connection with Spirit.

Dr Eric Pearl, Fred and Solomon and Lee Carroll and Kryon, thank you – for the work, the wisdom and the courage to bring it forth.

Huge hugs to Carol Mcbain and Dee Leamon. You were there at the very start and held the door open as I stepped into a different way of looking at the world.

Rik Schnabel – for your explanation of the mind from such a heart space. It's a magic mix and has been key in bringing this book to fruition.

Fellow travellers and dear friends, Lee Philips, Tracy Howard, Dee Rayson, Wayne Keogh, Lorelle Denham, Paula Blanda, Victoria Paris, Jayne and Hugh Briody, Dot and Manny, Kim, Rob, Tamika and Kyhani – thank you for the special part you each play in my life.

A huge thanks to Darren Stephens, Jackie Tallentyre and the entire Global Publishing team for your support and expertise during this process. Kelly, you were an angel and ever-patient with my many questions and the occasional meltdown.

Dave Gibb - thank you for your insight, amazing talent and pictures. It was a pleasure to meet the character that came from the little town of Dave's head. She made me laugh, blitzed the interview and got the job.

Mum and Dad – I'm forever grateful for all the love, encouragement and opportunity you gave me. Vicki, Linda, Glenn and Dean – there is no bond stronger than family and I'm honoured to be 'stuck' with you. Greg, Mick, Penny and Jacki – thank you for coming into and enriching our lives. To the young ones, Carly, Brent, Matthew, Tamara, Samantha and Jarod. It's a privilege to watch you grow and share in your lives. What they say is true – you help keep me young. And to the newest branch on the tree and youngest of all, Jett (Humpty) – your cheeky grin is like a glimpse into the future. I look at you with a sense of wonder at what lays ahead and what the future holds.

There are so many others. To list them all would be a book in its own right. To those not specifically mentioned I sincerely apologise and thank you from the bottom of my heart.

And to you – the reader. For your ongoing commitment to learn, grow and live an inspired life.

Enjoy the read.

Contents

Get on with It   103

About the Book

The information in this book will expand your mind. It looks at all aspects of change, not just the mechanical steps. You will become aware of your own power to make change which frees you to approach change from a very different perspective. As you take back control of creating your life, resistance and struggle around change dissolves. In three steps the Change Made Easy process shows you how to make change easy, enjoy the process and create the life you desire.

While I've covered theories and concepts in a simple manner please do not underestimate the potential of the information. It's based on the most up-to-date scientific findings.

There are references to explore the content at a deeper level if you choose but that is not necessary in order to get its benefits. Scientists make it their life's work. Spiritual Masters sit and meditate for years. I personally am happy to leave all of that to them and just benefit from their findings. Information from both sides of the fence now shows just how powerful we all are. An awareness of that and how to harness it makes for exciting times.

You can use this book in two ways. You may choose to simply read the book then return at a later time to apply the information and exercises in your life.

Or

Focus on a particular change you want to make as you read the book and apply the information and complete the exercises as you go. Either way is fine.

I imagine you already have a 'change list' somewhere, either stored in your mind or perhaps even written down. Those things in your life you'd like to change or have struggled to change. Perhaps there are things you would like to try for the very first time but have been putting off. Now is the perfect time to pick one thing that you'd like to play with as you go through the book. No, it's not a typo, I use the word 'play' intentionally. Change has been given a bad rap. The very mention of the word fills most people with a sense of dread. I think it's time to challenge that and, dare I say it, change the way we feel about making change.

Following the process outlined in the book gives you the opportunity to build a different relationship with change and see change in a new light. You will learn skills to embrace those changes you choose and be more accepting of ones that appear out of your control. You may even come to see that at times the only change you need is a change of perspective.

It's good practice to keep a journal when undertaking any program. It provides clarity, accountability and feedback. A journal allows you to review plans, make adjustments and also to track and celebrate your progress. I have created a workbook that accompanies the Change Made Easy process. You can access the template and track your progress by following the attached link or alternatively use an ordinary exercise book to record your change made easy journey.

Template link – www.ChangeMadeEasyBook.com/bonus

Introduction

It's a unique sense of frustration, a feeling like you're stuck knee deep in mud, wanting to move forward but unable to. Sometimes it comes from not knowing exactly what you want or where you want to go, at other times it's not knowing how to get there. Even more annoying is when you make some forward progress then find yourself slipping right back to where you started. Sound familiar? Hang in there.

Making effective, lasting change. Making it easily, with clarity and confidence. Regardless of what you want to change, this book gives you the formula. A simple three-stage process that makes it easy for you to move forward and achieve those things that until now have been hard work or always seemed just out of your reach. This information puts you back in control. It is a blueprint to identify what you want, to remove blocks and resistance and successfully make change.

The book has been written sequentially and consists of three stages. I suggest reading it from beginning to end to get its best effect. There are some exercises along the way to give you clarity and the opportunity to practically apply what's covered. Ultimately you will see that the actual process of change is easy and what normally makes things difficult is us getting in our own way.

Each time you see this symbol it indicates that it is your opportunity to complete an exercise to practically apply the change made easy process. This can be done in your downloaded workbook or in an exercise book you dedicate for that purpose.

The first stage looks at the nature of change, explores how you feel about making change, and what and why you want to change. This is an important part of the process that sets the scene for moving forward with clarity and focus. From this place of knowing and acceptance we move to stage two. Here we look at challenges and blocks that may have stopped you attempting or successfully making change. These could be external things such as knowledge or other services and resources. In most instances there's also something internal going on. You may know what that is but often it's hidden deep in your subconscious so you have no idea why you find change so challenging.

In this book I invite you to go on a journey of discovery. You will have the opportunity to look at your current circumstances from a very different perspective, without judgement, blame, shame or guilt. From that place, you can honestly consider what changes you would really like to make. What does your heart tell you? What changes more align you with your true, authentic nature? Those are the changes that bring a real sense of fulfilment. When considering any change, do so from your heart and listen to your intuition, that inner voice that knows the real you and what's in your best interest. Embrace the unique person that you are. Any change made in line with that will have you feeling energised, alive and on track.

The final stage of this change process is where the plan comes to life. It's when you see measurable results from taking steps towards your goal. Some people take baby steps, some sprint, while others take off and fly. However you choose to move forward is fine as even the smallest change in direction over time will bring you to a vastly different destination. One of the elements of making change easy is to enjoy the experience. You do that by designing a change plan with action steps that suit you.

While the information in this book is universal, its application will be as unique as each person who uses it. The process can be used time and time again and applied to any area of your life. For each one of you it has the potential to change the way you think about change, how you approach it, move through it and ultimately how you create your life.

Enjoy the read. Its pages are like a portal to opportunities and possibilities limited only by your imagination. It's time to choose what possibilities you want for yourself and to make the changes needed to achieve it. How can you do that? Easily, that's how.

GET REAL

*"It doesn't matter where you are,
you are nowhere compared to where you can go."*

– Bob Proctor

Authenticity

"What point is there in crossing the finish line first only to find you have run the wrong race?"
– Karen Wilson

To be authentic is to be real and genuine. Merriam-Webster dictionary describes authenticity as: *True to one's own personality, spirit, or character.*

So are you living authentically? Are you doing what you really want to do with your life? Do your thoughts, words and actions support a life you genuinely want to live? It's a very rare person who follows the conviction of their heart. If that person is you, congratulations. Most people spend a large portion of their lives living according to others beliefs, rules and expectations. Sadly some people live their entire lives that way, never checking in with what they would really like and then following their heart.

For some it's been so long since they even considered what they'd really like they struggle to know just what that is. I'd like you to take a few moments here to consider this for yourself. Why you ask? Well, we are in the business of making change and as you learn a simple process to do that I want you to make change that inspires you and for you to live an authentic life that you love.

There is a beautiful short video on YouTube that gave members of the public in New York the opportunity to write on a chalk board what their biggest regret was.* The common thread in this showed the thing people regret most was *not* doing something that was significant to them. Check out the video. It takes about three and a half minutes. And now spend a minute to reflect on your biggest regret. If you were walking past that board right now, what would you write? Right here and now is the perfect opportunity for you to check in with things you have been putting off or struggled to do and then make it happen. Here's to not only making change easy but to living a life without regrets.

* http:/aplus.com/a/clean-slate-blackboard-experiment

The Nature of Change

> *"There is never nothing going on."*
> – Dan Millman

As you begin the journey to unlock your potential for change, let's take a moment to look at the nature of change. Perhaps the easiest way to do this is by looking at nature itself. Things are forever moving and shifting. Change is ongoing and happening locally, globally and beyond.

Each year, time rolls on and we watch the seasons come and go. Further afield, Astronomers use powerful telescopes to study changes in the skies and report the birth of new stars. Closer to home, through the technology of ultrasound, expectant parents see the changes and development of their child even before it is born. Change is the most natural thing in the world and is fundamental to life.

While ultimately a change in one thing has an impact on all things this book is focused on the individual and making personal change. Did you know that every second of your life millions of cells die and are replaced in your body. Over a period of approximately seven years your body will have completely replaced itself – how's that for change!

In the context of our own lives change is occurring all the time, all around us and within us. It's ironic really that change is such a naturally occurring thing yet when we choose to make a particular change we often find it difficult and struggle to do so. Why is that?

One of the main reasons we struggle with change stems from a naturally occurring response to change that's hardwired in our brains. It exists to keep us safe and comfortable and creates resistance to new or unknown things. This response has many faces that sit and huddle under an umbrella we call fear. It is responsible for our emotions and behaviours that get in the way when we set about making a change.

While this response is an issue and needs to be addressed, it's important that we don't throw out the baby with the bathwater. This fear response is still appropriate if we find ourselves in real physical danger. The issue is that our triggers for fear have been distorted. We've learnt to be fearful of so many things and to such a degree that our fear response works overtime. Often working behind the scenes at a subconscious level it springs into action thinking it's protecting us when there is no real danger. All it achieves by doing this is to paralyse us and prevent us from making change, experiencing new things and creating the life we desire.

This ability our mind has to jump to our defence is a sign of our own amazing design. We have a brilliant brain that responds instantly to something it believes is a threat. It is so responsive and protective that it reacts regardless of if the threat is real or not. Simply recalling a challenging situation will cause it to respond. Imagining or anticipating challenges in new or future situations will also trigger this response to come to our aid. So with the best of intentions, our own defence mechanisms are often the underlying cause of a lot of the struggle we experience around change. We will look more at this in the second section of the book where you will develop a new relationship with fear. With an awareness of how fear operates in your life you can create a new connection to it and use the response it generates to energise and propel you forward rather than hold you back.

As change is a natural and constant part of life it makes sense to learn to embrace it rather than resist it. You can no sooner opt out and keep things as they are than you can stop the tide coming in. Crossing your fingers and calling 'barley' may have worked when playing the child's game of Tiggy but will not halt life's progress. Resistance to the natural flow of life only creates a source of stress that can hinder change and have a huge impact on your life.

Do you know what your struggles are around change and where they come from? As you work through the Change Made Easy process you will come to understand this (and yourself) much more. With that awareness and understanding you are positioned to let go of the struggle and experience change in a very different way. Don't be fooled. While the Change Made Easy process has been simplified into three steps the results it produces can be far reaching. It has the potential to change the way you create and experience your life.

In following the process you embark on a journey of discovery. It's an exploration of your life as you know it, of the life you desire and the amazing capacity you have to create it. As all things are connected, regardless of any one change you make, following this process is powerful and can produce change that ripples out across all areas of your life.

> *"To become more conscious is the greatest gift anyone can give to the world; moreover, in a ripple effect, the gift comes back to its source."*
>
> **– David Hawkins**

We will get to the simple three-stage process to make change shortly. Spending some time first to understand the underlying ingredients of change is essential to the Change Made Easy process. Science now knows that our own personal reality is dependent on what's going on in our mind. I have touched on just how powerful your mind is at creating blocks to change. Those emotions and behaviours it creates in the belief it's keeping us safe. The good news is that the mind is just as powerful at creating change. Once you know how to harness its incredible power you can direct that power to work for you. That includes making change and creating the things you would like in your life. Your mind holds the key. All change starts there. All creation starts there.

Before we go any further I think it's timely to point something out. If you want to change your current circumstances you are going to need to do something differently. To attempt change without that embodies Albert Einstein's famous definition of insanity, which is to do the same thing over and over again and expect a different result.

And so it begins. As we start this journey together the most important thing you can bring to the table is an open mind. It's not only desirable, it's essential. The mind you currently have is the same mind that has caused the struggle with change. Since we're all about giving up the struggle and making change easier it will be at the level of your mind that we get to play. Let's call it a play date. With an open mind and a playful Spirit I think you will be amazed at what you can achieve.

Creatures of Habit

"Some people live ninety-nine years while others live one year ninety-nine times."

– Unknown

It's true what they say, we are creatures of habit. It is actually a reflection of how brilliant our minds are and for the most part serves us well. Most of us go about our day without giving it much thought. If you don't believe me, next time you get out of the shower, do something as simple as dry yourself in reverse. Hold the towel in your opposite hand and start drying on a different part of your body. Does it feel strange? Is it awkward? Do you need to concentrate on what you're doing? Perhaps it takes you longer. All because you are not following your normal habit. You have disrupted the automatic pattern you have for 'getting dry'. Well, I'll let you in on a little secret, we have patterns for how we do everything. Our entire lives are lived by running patterns. These patterns cover not only what we do but also how we think and feel about things. With a large percentage of them stored in our subconscious we go about our daily lives thinking, acting and feeling according to these patterns, often with no logical understanding of why we think, act or feel the way we do.

So how do we learn and lock in a pattern to the point where it becomes a habit? Something becomes a habit when we repeat it to the point where it becomes our norm. Firstly it's important that you understand we have two levels of mind, our conscious and subconscious. The following learning cycle shows how habits are created and stored at the subconscious level.

The four stages of learning:

1. Unconscious incompetence

2. Conscious incompetence

3. Conscious competence

4. Unconscious competence

We move from the first stage where we are not even aware that we're unskilled to stage two where we understand that our skill is lacking. From there, with instruction and repetition we move to the third stage where with focus and attention we are able to demonstrate a skill proficiently. Eventually you reach the fourth stage you when you have mastered the skill and are running the pattern (be that a thought, word, emotion or action) without thinking about it. The pattern has become a habit that you do unconsciously.

Recall when you learnt to drive a car. Initially the car jumped and stalled while you mastered the art of changing gears. Gradually you learnt to change gears smoothly and stopped almost going through the windscreen as you learnt to judge the brakes. In time and with enough practice most people are able to drive a car, sing along to the radio, decide what to wear to work the next day and plan what's for dinner all at the same time. Being able to multitask like this is essential in the fast-paced world we live in today.

So what do habits have to do with making change? Our ability to store and run patterns unconsciously serves us well in many ways. Can you imagine having to focus on every task you did each day as if attempting it for the first time? Life as we know it would be impossible. Scientists say that most of our communication is unconscious. Our conscious brains can only handle approximately 40 bits of information a second, while our subconscious minds take in up to 11 million bits of information per second. With data like this the benefits of selective attention and running patterns on autopilot is obvious.

Over time we accumulate and lock in patterns at a subconscious level that cover every area of our life. The foundations for how we experience life are largely laid down when we are children. From birth to the age of seven is known as the imprint years. During this time our brains have virtually no filter and are like sponges. Everything the child sees, hears, feels or is exposed to is absorbed at a subconscious level as real. This information becomes the framework or the points of reference that run in the background for a person as they grow up. It is where our original values and beliefs come from.

By the age of 30 most of us have locked in patterns and habits to cover almost any situation we will encounter. Pretty amazing really. So for the most part we go about our day efficiently, not needing to think about each and everything we do. Routine things basically take care of themselves without needing our focus. This automated way of living works fine until we want to do something different and change some aspect of our lives. Then you may find that those subconscious programs running in the background that helped make your life cruisy until now may be the very things that make change difficult or keep you stuck.

An essential part of the Change Made Easy process is to check in on these patterns to ensure they support your change. When you say you want a change that is your conscious mind speaking. If your subconscious mind is running patterns that don't support that change, things can be difficult if not impossible. We explore this more in part two of the book. For now it's enough that you're aware of the two parts of your mind and understand that conflict between the conscious and subconscious can cause problems.

The Neutral Zone

"The ability to observe without evaluating is the highest form of intelligence."
— Jiddu Krishnamurti

Are you ready to free up some energy and enthusiasm to put towards making change? Applying this one thing will give you an energy boost, ignite your enthusiasm and fuel your motivation to move toward and reach goals. So where might these hidden gems of change be hiding? One word with an enormous capacity to store, conceal and trap our potential to change is judgement.

The amount of energy we spend in judgement is staggering. Remember we spoke about changing things in order to change how we do change? Well, here's a biggie. From this point forward as you work through this process I ask you to put aside all negative judgement. What does that mean? Things like blame, shame, guilt, resentment and anger. Regardless of if we go there towards ourselves or others these toxic states rob us of our energy, our creativity and motivation. They achieve nothing other than weighing you down and sapping your joy of life. Like a glue this negativity may be keeping you stuck and making change difficult.

When it comes to self-criticism, if you are like most people you're probably your own worst enemy. It's often said that if you spoke to others the way you speak to yourself you would be a very lonely person. No one would (or should) tolerate the criticism that you heap on yourself. "I'm such an idiot. God, I'm stupid. I stuffed up again. I can't do anything right." Sound familiar?

Unleashing energy that has until now been tied up in judgement is a really important part of laying the foundation for Change Made Easy. Ultimately, letting go of judgement is a wonderful way to do life but for now I would like your commitment to at least apply this principle to your concept of change. It may feel strange (because it's different) but stay with me, play with me and let's do this!

We are going to create a neutral zone. This will be your dedicated space where all change occurs. Negative judgement has no place here. Every change you undertake is an experience that produces a result. In your neutral zone outcomes will be what they will be and there is no negativity attached to the result. By merely noticing the outcome from the neutral zone you are in a position to decide how you would like to move forward.

Is it an experience you would like to repeat? If not, what would you like to try next? If you had an outcome in mind did your actions achieve that outcome? If yes, are you now going to move forward to something else? If not, do you still want to achieve the original outcome you wanted? If so, what will you do differently next time in order to achieve or move closer to that outcome? This way of experiencing change and indeed life builds incredible resilience.

So go ahead and create your neutral zone now. Picture it in your mind. How do you move into the zone? Is it a space you visualise and imagine stepping into? If it is, how big and what shape is it? Perhaps your neutral zone is accessed through your breathing. You may see your neutral zone as a bathtub where all negativity simply drains away while you soak in warm sudsy water. Personalise your zone. What about a comfortable chair where you sit and review things? Whatever works for you. This is your space, your zone.

Now to get the hang of this let's try your neutral zone out. Think of something that holds a negative charge for you. Perhaps it's someone you believed wronged you or a time when you felt hard done by. You may even like to use a situation you've been beating yourself up about. As you think of that incident now step into your neutral zone. As you do this decide how you intend to release any negativity? Does it drain from the bath? If you've stepped into a particular space is there a force field that prevents negativity entering? In your neutral zone does any negativity simply float away like a helium balloon? Perhaps you have a laser beam that shatters and disintegrates any negativity. If your focus is on breathing does negativity get released each time you breathe out? Get creative and find a way that is fun, dynamic and easy to dissolve and release any negativity.

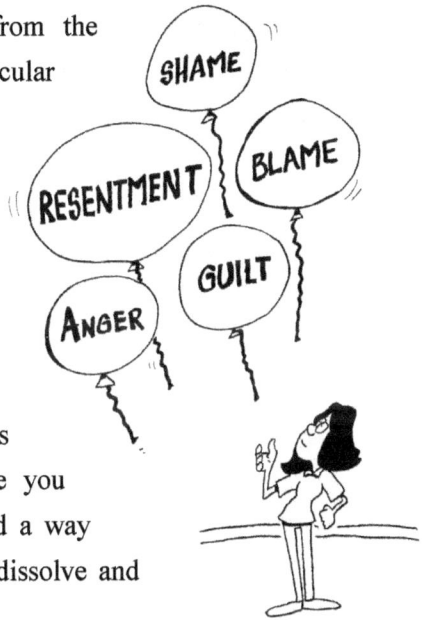

If you initially find it challenging to let go of negative energy, do this. It's like the icing on the cake of your neutral zone. Shift your attention from your head or wherever in your body you hold the negativity and allow it to move down into your heart. This is my personal favourite. With each breath I just allow any negative feelings or thoughts to move to the central chest area. As I breathe into my heart any negativity I send there simply dissolves and is gone. I will talk about the intelligence of the heart a bit later on. For now just know that it is a powerful filter to dissipate any negativity.

By approaching change in this way energy that was previously tied up in judgment (of yourself and others) is released. Instead of holding you back that energy is now available to help you move forward and make change easily. Initially this may feel strange, almost as if something is missing. That's good! It indicates you're disrupting your old habits and patterns of judgement around change. You're laying the foundations for the Change Made Easy process. Judgement has been red-carded and sent off the field. Your neutral zone is a key player that you definitely want on your team – lock it in.

The Mechanics of Change

> *"In order to seek one's own direction, one must simplify the mechanics of ordinary, everyday life."*
>
> **– Plato**

Are you ready? I'm going to spell out the three simple stages to make any change. Here they are:

1. **Get Real**

   · Determine where you currently are (point A).

   · Define where you want to go to (point B).

2. **Get Ready**

   · Identify the steps required to move from point A to B.

   · Remove any blocks that may impede your progress.

3. **Get on with it**

   · Take action and move from A to B.

The book has been set out to follow this exact process. So if the entire change process can be summarised in a couple of lines what's the point of the rest of the book? If it's that simple why aren't we all just sailing through life, making shifts and changes without hiccups, hurdles or heartache? Well, while the mechanics of change really is that simple, we are a bit more complex. We are capable of amazing things. Scientists' are now able to map the incredible activity of our brains. How it learns, records and recalls things. Forget space or the depths of the oceans. The greatest frontier of our time, the place that holds incredible untapped potential is a lot closer to home – the human brain. The Change Made Easy process uses cutting-edge scientific principles to change the way you use your brain. It also looks at the 'stuff' we've been carrying around as often that is what gets in the way, muddies the waters and makes change more challenging.

So in this book we will be looking at our 'stuff'. Now don't panic. People often find this type of thing off-putting. "What, look at what's going on in my mind? I'm fine. There is nothing wrong with me."

And you're right. There is absolutely nothing wrong with you. But with all the new knowledge around about how our brains work, wouldn't you like to make the best use of its amazing capacity? Think about technology. When mobile phones first came out they were affectionately known as a brick. For those of you too young to remember that's because they were about the same size as a house brick. I bet that even if they were still available not too many of you would choose to lug around the original model. While it was revolutionary at the time, by today's standards it was bulky, heavy and had limited functions. As technology advances phones become less cumbersome, lighter and capable of so much more. It's pretty much the same with our brains. Not that our brains have changed so much but rather we now have a better understanding of it. So are you ready to upgrade your brain? The Change Made Easy program will help you do that. And just like the phone upgrade, upgrading your brain allows you to harness and direct your mind's immense potential to work smarter and function at a whole new level.

Some of the information in the book may push your buttons. That's actually a good thing. It's an indicator that you are encountering new information and concepts. These are the ingredients you will use to do things in new and different ways. Remember you need to do something different in order to produce a different outcome. That requires you to expand your way of thinking and be open to new possibilities. Any apprehension or scepticism that starts to surface is just your protection response kicking into gear. If that happens I want you to just notice and acknowledge it then move into your neutral zone. From there simply use one of the techniques you practised earlier and allow any negativity to dissolve or be released.

While I've intentionally designed the book to be an easy read, the principles it covers are profound. Each person who reads the book will take something different from it. Take what's right for you, apply it, and not only will you make change easy, you will change the course of your life.

Every experience you have adds to the tapestry of your life. Occasionally there may be one particular point or event that stands out as a pivotal stepping stone. One such point for me occurred 17 years ago when I was drawn to study reflexology. This is a complementary wellness modality that's based on the premise that there are reflex points on the feet, hands and ears that correspond to all of our body organs and systems. Applying pressure to these reflex points stimulates the body to come back into balance assisting overall better health and any healing required.

On day one of the course people stood around chatting using words like meridian lines, chakras and metaphysics. I had absolutely no idea what they were talking about and felt like a fish out of water. I thought what on earth have I let myself in for and wanted to run a mile. Had I not already paid a significant amount of money up front for the two-year course I would have done just that. It was new, it was different, and far too airy-fairy for my predominately scientific mind. Not one to waste a sizable chunk of change I stuck it out and in doing so made some amazing friendships and gained insights that changed the way I view my world.

This study was the catalyst that led me down a path of exploring human behaviour and potential. And so it continues. For over 17 years I have read, researched and studied. My mind has been opened and expanded with a combination of scientific principles and Spiritual phenomenon. It's a powerful mix. I have experienced first-hand just how easily we are able to change and create our life when we know how. This book and the Change Made Easy process contains that information for you. Who knows, perhaps in time you will look back and recognise it was a pivotal stepping-stone for you.

We are living at a very exciting time when science and Spirituality blend beautifully in the study of our human potential. We arrive in this world, in this physical expression we call our bodies, but nowhere in the packaging do we have instructions. Scientists are now able to measure the amazing potential that exists in each and every one of us and the incredible power of our thoughts, words and emotions. These intangible things are now proven to impact on our physical bodies, our mental health and individual experience of our world. Quantum physics will go one further and say not only do they affect our world but they actually create the world we live in. If they are that powerful, surely it's worth looking at their role in making change.

So you see that while we're certainly going to look at the

traditional mechanics of making change we will be going a lot further than that. The Change Made Easy process goes behind the scenes, or should I say under the bonnet, to get to the inner workings of yourself. When all is said and done we are not that different from a car that runs smoother and more economically with a well-tuned engine, the right tyre pressure and a grease and oil change. Hand me that spanner will you!

Pure Potential

Our deepest fear is not that we are inadequate.

Our deepest fear is that we are powerful beyond measure.

It is our light not our darkness that most frightens us.

We ask ourselves, who am I to be brilliant, gorgeous, talented and fabulous?

Actually, who are you not to be? You are a child of God.

Your playing small does not serve the world.

There's nothing enlightened about shrinking so that other people won't feel insecure around you.

We were born to make manifest the glory of God that is within us.

It's not just in some of us; it's in everyone.

And as we let our own light shine we unconsciously give other people permission to do the same.

As we are liberated from our own fear our presence automatically liberates others.

– Marianne Williamson

Do you know how powerful you are? It's one of my favourite things – to witness someone become aware of their own potential. Years ago when I first read Marianne Williamson's words I caught my breath. It was like someone had thrown cold water in my face. Reading the words I felt like was playing hide and seek and had just been caught out.

There is a groundswell of people who recognise they are here to do more than they currently are with their lives. Marianne's words point this out beautifully from a Spiritual perspective. While each person's connection to Marianne's words will be unique, the underlying message encourages you to grow, to shine and live your life fully. The ability to embrace and make change is pivotal to doing that.

If Marianne's words provide the why, science is now able to provide the how. With advanced scientific understanding of how the brain works we are able to harness the power it has to make change and create. And that ability is huge. As you upgrade to a new level of mind you access a source of pure potential that you can direct to create the things you want.

Your thoughts, words and emotions are the foundation of any change you intend. They are like gold nuggets that contain dormant potential. It's amazing how powerful these intangible things are. Every thought, word and emotion you have has its own specific energy. Dependent on those you choose they can be working for you or against you. The Change Made Easy process develops your awareness of this principle and allows you to make choices that support your change.

In years gone by the ability to create unexplained change or to manifest things was seen as coincidence or even some form of magic. Today science has given up the magicians secrets. It is within each one of us to create and sculpt the life we want for ourselves. And you guessed it, thoughts, words and emotions play a large part.

Here are just a few different examples of studies and work done by people around that:

Dr David Hawkins used kinesiology and muscle testing in his book *Power vs. Force*. In it he created a numerical scale to represent the energy associated with various emotions. His book looks at how the energy of each person affects not only the individual but also the collective. If you're not familiar with muscle testing – Google it. There are a number of YouTubes that demonstrate this process much clearer than I can describe it. It is a simple and effective tool you can use in your own life on a daily basis. It allows you to test if a statement or question is true or false by muscle testing the energy attached to what is said. This can be applied to almost any area of your life. I've used it to find misplaced items, to check if products on supermarket shelves are suitable for me and to get clarity around decisions I make.

The science of epigenetics includes the study of how your health, wellness and the very expression of your genes is affected by your environment. Epigenetics means above or over genes. It is an additional layer of instructions that controls how your DNA is interpreted — how your genes are controlled and expressed. In his book, *The Biology of Belief,* Dr Bruce Lipton looks at how the environment you put yourself in has implications not only in basic cell development but also in disease and other physical conditions.

The environment you live in is made up of many different elements. It includes external things like where you live and the conditions you live in. People and circumstances you surround yourself with and what you invest your time in like work and hobbies are also included. From there we move to your internal environment. This is forever shifting and changing depending on your mental and emotional state. The nutrition you provide your body is just as important. All of these things combine to create your environment which is showing out scientifically to have a huge impact on your experience of life.

Dr Masaru Emoto was an author, researcher and photographer who captured the effect that thoughts and words, (written and spoken) had on water. His pictures revealed the impact that the energy of a thought or word from one source had on another. Dr Emoto would expose a sample of water to a word and then freeze a drop of that water. As that droplet was thawed pictures were taken using special photographic equipment. The following photos show how drops exposed to an empowering word such as love or gratitude revealed beautifully formed crystals. Drops exposed to words such as hate and anger produced distorted malformed crystals.

I love you.

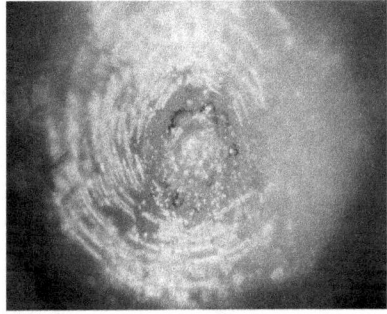

You fool.

I want you to think about this. Dependent on your age, gender and body composition your body consists of anywhere between 50–65% of water. If exposure to the energy of just one word has the power to produce such a pronounced change in a single drop of water, how much of an impact are your thoughts, words and emotions having on you?

I know we're spending quite a bit of time on this mind stuff and I make no apologies for that. An awareness of the importance it plays in making change is essential to the Change Made Easy process. Start to become aware of your own thoughts as you read this book. How does the information make you feel? Are you saying anything to yourself? Become the observer of your own reactions. This awareness and ability to observe is the starting point for identifying and letting go of any thoughts, words and emotions that are not working for you. Journal anything that stands out about your experience. In reflection it can make for fascinating reading.

To Play or Play it Safe

> *"And the day came when the risk to remain tight in a bud was more painful than the risk it took to blossom."*
> – Anais Nin

I know how disheartening the struggle with change can be. Feeling overwhelmed, frustrated and ultimately disappointed was an emotional pattern I ran for years around 'failed' change. However it plays out for you personally I know that struggling with change is off-putting and dampens your enthusiasm for life. Rather than be disappointed again it's tempting to play it safe. If you're not careful you may find yourself being a spectator of your own life. Well, life was not designed to be a spectator sport. It's time to get off the bench and back in the game.

As you work through the Change Made Easy process, you will be installing patterns and habits that support you achieve what you want. Regardless of what your challenge has been around change in the past and how that has affected you, things are about to change. It's time to get enthusiastic about your life again. As you upgrade your brain see yourself back in control of your life, sitting in the driver's seat and looking out at all the possibilities ahead of you. And right there beside you, strapped into the passenger seat and keen to get started on the next chapter of your life journey is a key player on your team, enthusiasm. Embrace it and enjoy its company as you move forward.

I believe the best way to honour the gift of life we have been given is by living a full and rich life. Let's face it, if you want to sit wrapped in cotton wool, breathing purified air and eating only macrobiotic food you may live to be hundreds of years old but who would want to? A life devoid of connection, experiences and growth is merely an existence. Even a pool of pure water will stagnate if left still for too long. We are designed to explore, engage, grow and evolve.

When we are young, growth is more prevalent and obvious. Children get bigger. They learn to walk, to speak and develop other basic motor skills. We experience so many 'firsts' when we are young. Below is a list of some general milestones most people reach before the age of 21. What else do you remember doing for the first time when you were young?

FIRSTS:

- Birthday party
- School
- Ride on a bike
- Boyfriend/Girlfriend
- Ride in a train
- Taste of different foods

- Visit to the dentist
- Drove a car
- Movie
- Sense of confidence
- Heartbreak
- Pet
- Voted

- Job
- Visit to the zoo
- Drank alcohol
- Graduated
- Music concert
- Day at the beach
- Sense of failure

It's impossible to recall all of the firsts we've ever had. Everything we've known, felt or experienced had a first at some point. Based on our experiences all these firsts eventually lead to those patterns stored in our subconscious that create our habits and behaviours today. While these patterns may not be obvious at first glance their impact is huge. They are like a pair of glasses you wear to view your world or the little voice that whispers in your ear. They may have been running in the background on autopilot for many years.

In order to switch the autopilot off it's necessary to acknowledge, access and examine your existing patterns. Doing this is how you take back control of your life. From here you are able to look at things in new ways and make different choices. You get to create new patterns that serve you and assist you make change. Ultimately you can reprogram the autopilot to take you to your desired destination and also upgrade to first class for the journey. Now that sounds like a change worth making!

My observation is that as people get older, a large percentage go about their day like they're sleep-walking or living their own personal version of the movie *Groundhog Day*. I've touched on the way that habits and patterns influence our lives and assist us to multitask. While that's all well and good I think that as people age they often live such automated lives that they become desensitised to the beauty of life that is all around them and forget to continue to include firsts. Where is it written that getting older means the loss of enthusiasm or wonder for life? It's not!

One way to re-engage with life in a fresh and new way is to see your world through the eyes of a child. It's lots of fun to do and extremely entertaining. As the Change Made Easy process involves looking at change in a new way this is something I suggest you do as you go through the book. It will encourage you to play with your life, take pleasure in the simple things and celebrate your accomplishments. Being childlike involves being present and aware of things around you. Incredible resilience is also the hallmark of a child. These traits served you well when you were young and will do so again as you re-establish your relationship with change.

If you find the concept of being childlike with your life a bit flippant perhaps you'd prefer to think of yourself as an explorer or scientist. The explorer is fearless and loves new experiences. Explorers approach change as an adventure and go boldly to discover new horizons. The scientist is much more clinical. Remaining detached from outcomes and viewing endeavours and results in a factual, analytical manner is the way the scientist does change.

A truly rich life is full of adventures, experiments and exploration. Choosing a character to identify with will help you get past any resistance to new information you encounter. It will encourage you to look at things in a new and novel way. For the purpose of the exercise just imagine you're selecting a player piece for a board game. Are you the child, the explorer or the scientist? It's your life, you choose.

Choose your character and enjoy the game of 'Change Made Easy'.

> *"All life is an experiment.*
> *The more experiments you make the better."*
> **– Ralph Waldo Emerson**

As you move forward keep in mind that any memorable ride has a wow factor of some type. And so it is with life. All the twists and turns, the ups and downs and surprises you encounter are part of the ride. It's what gives life its depth and colour. With any change, as with life, you may encounter highs, lows and the unexpected. It's all part of the journey and perfectly natural. Your experience of change will depend on how you respond to these things. So far you have your neutral zone, your chosen character and enthusiasm on board as your companions for this ride you're on.

As you create your remarkable life they will encourage you to embrace change, seek it out and move through it with a smile rather than a grimace. When you do that you will surely succeed at life regardless of circumstances or outcomes.

I love this quote about a life fully lived. I've taken the liberty of changing it and added two of my favourites, chocolate and ouzo. As you reflect on the wonderland that is this planet and all the experiences it offers, consider, what might you be holding as you slide into home plate?

> "Life should not be a journey to the grave with the intention of arriving safely in a pretty and well preserved body, but rather to skid in broadside, in a cloud of smoke, chocolate in one hand ouzo in the other, thoroughly used up, totally worn out, and loudly proclaiming "Wow! What a Ride!"
>
> – Hunter S. Thompson,
> *The Proud Highway: Saga of a Desperate Southern Gentleman, 1955–1967*

Clarity

"Anyone who has ever asked for directions knows you need two crucial pieces of information to get good results: a starting point and a destination."

— Mike Quigley

It's time to take stock of things as they currently are. To evaluate your current circumstances and establish your starting point. Remember to play by your new rules. Judgment sits this one out.

If you've ever worked in retail the term 'stock take' may conjure up images of staying late and endless counting and cross-checking actual stock against stock lists. For the customer hearing 'stock take' may hold the promise of huge savings and finding that item you've always wanted at a great discount. For you, in terms of making change, doing your own personal stock take is essential. By taking stock of your current circumstances you become both the retailer and customer of your own life. Knowing what 'stock' you currently carry allows you to make informed decisions on where you'd like to go from there. It gives you a clear starting point to choose what you want to keep on the shelves, what you'll let go of and what you would like to order in as you move forward.

So let's just think about that for a moment. If all the elements of your life were the 'stock' in your 'life store':

- What are your best sellers?

- What stuff looks good on the shelf but just sits there and makes no profit?

- Do you have old stock taking up shelf space that used to sell well but it's just no longer in vogue?

- Are you carrying stock that is out of date?

- And what about all those returns you have stashed away out in the back room? Those things that were faulty, have missing parts or are broken? Chances are that back room is full of stuff you've completely forgotten about.

People are more relaxed, creative and productive in a space that supports that. This makes sense and is obvious in our external environment. A pleasant, functional space, free of clutter, is a much nicer place to spend time and more conducive to getting things done. There are businesses dedicated to decluttering houses and work spaces to improve productivity, creativity and wellbeing.

The same principle applies to our internal environment yet people often overlook doing a stock take there. It's a mistake that can cost you dearly and often why people struggle or fail to achieve their dreams. When was the last time you took the time to check if your internal environment was supporting you? This is part of the Change Made Easy process. You will get to keep those things that are working for you and discard the ones that aren't. You also get the opportunity to order in new things that look and feel great, sell well and assist you achieve the life you desire.

Yardsticks

> *"The privilege of a lifetime is to become who you truly are."*
> – C.G. Jung

In the process of determining what you want to change, have you ever stopped to consider why you want what you want? What makes you want a particular thing or goal? It's important to take a closer look at this as part of the change process. After all, why go about making a change unless it's something you really want. While any change is possible, change for the sake of change may leave you feeling dissatisfied even after you achieve it.

Often the things we aspire to and spend a significant amount of time to achieve are not what we know in our hearts we really want. So why would anyone live anything other than a truly authentic life? I like to call them yardsticks. They come at us from all angles. Family, friends, school, society, careers and partners. They are things perceived as a measure of our worth and include things like achievements, appearance and acquisitions. Below is a list of just some:

- Own your own home
- Have a nice home
- Be gainfully employed
- Get the promotion
- Make good money
- Be financially secure
- Own a nice car
- Be in a relationship
- Be married
- Be happily married
- Have children
- Be well travelled
- Have a good level of education
- Successful career

- Physically fit
- Correct weight
- Physically appealing
- White teeth
- Nice clothes
- Great hair
- Be popular

How do you measure up? It's human nature to want to feel like you belong and to be accepted. The risk is that in the effort to be acceptable in the eyes of others you can lose sight of what's really important to you. The authentic you is lost as you spend your time striving to meet the yardsticks and benchmarks of others.

This can come at a very high price. Measuring your own self-worth by constantly comparing yourself to others is somewhat like living your entire life running one continuous never-ending marathon. It becomes a competition, an ongoing race to see who is able to acquire more, achieve more and or course look stunning in the process. Exhausting!

The Change Made Easy process is the perfect opportunity to consider if a chosen change supports the authentic you, or is just part of a quest to measure up.

No one else is watching, now is the time to be honest. Remember this section of the book is called 'get real'. Do you feel the need to achieve some things because it's expected of you or in order to be accepted by others rather than it being something you really want?

Take a moment to consider what your authentic life might look like? What is it that puts a smile on your face and makes your heart sing? If you didn't give two hoots about what anyone else thought of you, what choices would you make then? What would you really like to change in your life? Changes made in line with that are ones you'll be enthusiastic about, truly enjoy making and find a real sense of fulfilment in achieving.

Instead of living by yardsticks, try living by your sticks. Put your stick in the ground and declare one thing you intend to change to move into alignment with your most authentic self. Always remember that the measure of your life is not how you stack up against anyone else because you are not like anyone else, you are unique. In the future when considering any change reflect on your reasons for wanting it and choose change that supports your authenticity.

> 'Everybody is a genius. But if you judge a fish by it's ability to climb a tree, it will live its whole life believing that it is stupid.'
>
> **– Albert Einstein**

Now if you're like me and have a number of things on your radar to change, relax, we are all a work in progress. That's exactly as it should be. You were born to continue to learn, grow and evolve. For now pick just one. Whatever your chosen change, the very first step in the Change Made Easy process is to identify and be accepting of where you're starting from.

So let's establish your point 'A'. Stand in your neutral zone and just notice the circumstance of your life you would like to change. What got you here is irrelevant. It is what it is. In the Change Made Easy process you direct your energy, attention and focus on moving forward towards your desired outcome. From your neutral zone I want you to look at it from all directions. Walk around it, over it, under it and without emotion take note of those circumstances and also why you want to make a change here.

For example, if you were looking to improve your financial situation, specific elements of your current reality may be:

- $2000 dollars in debt on credit card.

- Car payments overdue.

- $550,000 mortgage.

- Owe parents $5000.

The reason you want to make a change in this area of your life could include things like:

- Paying extremely high interest on money owed on credit card.

- Afraid the car will be repossessed.

- Feeling like a prisoner in your own home trying to make mortgage repayments.

- Feeling guilty about owing parents money.

- Frustrated at having no money for social life or holidays.

- Embarrassed that finances have reached this point.

If the type of change you're focusing on relates more to an internal state such as reducing anxiety the specific elements around that may look something like this:

- I'm withdrawn and avoid social situations.

- I'm tired due to poor sleep.

- I'm scared others will judge me for feeling this way.

- I'm embarrassed by the way this anxiety grips me.

- I worry obsessively over things.

- I feel physically ill.

- I'm not in a relationship.

- I often miss work.

Reasons you may like to reduce your anxiety could include:

- To enjoy socialising with family and friends.

- To sleep well and wake refreshed.

- To enjoy good health

- To feel in control of your thoughts and body.

- To enjoy life and be able to relax.

- To find a partner.

- To be considered for promotion.

If your old friend judgement pops its head up while you do this just send it straight back to the bench. Remember, judgement is no longer on the team. It's just keen to get back on the field because that's the habit and pattern you used to run. Approach your circumstances in a factual way and just say it as it is. Go to your neutral zone to dissolve and release any negativity.

Now it's your turn. Put your stick in the ground and declare one thing you intend to change. Go to your workbook and journal your starting point (point A) now.

Your point A consists of two lists. After identifying the change you want to make write down the specific elements of your current circumstances around that in the first list. Break it down and be as specific as you can. You can always come back to this list and add or amend it later should you wish. These are the facts of your current situation.

The second list around your change contains the reasons why you want to make this change. Things listed hear may be factual but often will include emotional reasons. This list shows how the elements in the first list are affecting your life and what impact they're having. Again, break it down and list as many specific reasons as possible.

Now beside your second list (for those using the template) you will see some columns. In the first column I want you to write a number between 0–10. This number represents how much of an impact that point is having on your life right now. 0 means no impact at all, right through to 10 being a massive impact on your life. Fill that column in now for each reason you have listed (or write it in your exercise book). The extra columns should be completed each week when you review your plan. This is a way of measuring the progress you are making and checking to what degree, if any, what you are working on is still impacting your life.

Well done! You have nominated a change to make. It has been examined without judgement, you've identified its specific elements and listed the reasons you seek to make this particular change.

Your point 'A' has been established.

Destination

> *"If you don't know where you are going; you'll probably end up somewhere else."*
>
> – Lewis Carroll

Before you order the stock for your new life store it's important to have a very clear vision for the business. Having established your starting point the next step is to determine where you're going. What do you really want? What is your destination? Taking time to get clear on what you want is time well spent. If you skip this step you may find yourself going around and around in circles and getting nowhere or seeing change but not achieving the particular change you wanted.

In line with making change easy it's important you are able to direct your energy, attention and focus on something you have clearly defined. Let's establish your point 'B'. So, what is it you want? What one specific change have you decided to work with as you go through the book? In establishing your starting point you wrote the current circumstances around that and why you want to make the change.

In defining your destination you need to be able to recognise when you've achieved it. How will you know when you've arrived? What does it look like to have successfully made your change?

If I continue with the previous example of wanting an improved financial situation it may look like this:

- Credit card paid off.

- Own a more affordable car.

- Mortgage restructured to manageable payments.

- Parents paid back money owed.

- Enjoying being in control my life and finances.

If I imagine how achieving the change might play out in my life it may look something like this.

- I use my credit card to pay for airport parking as we pull into catch our flights to Fiji. The card is debt free and used for convenience only. Mum is so excited to be coming along. I have gifted her the trip in appreciation for the money she loaned me some time back that I have fully repaid. My new car is fantastic. Smaller and more economical than the old one, I'm able to handle the repayments and it's so much cheaper to run. I've restructured my mortgage so I have money available for socialising and the occasional holiday. It feels so good to be back in control of my money. I feel lighter, breathe easier and smile more often. Watching the planes taking off and landing gives me butterflies. I can smell the plane fuel. It's a typical Melbourne day, overcast, cold and windy and I get goose bumps as I stand and wait for the car park bus. "We will have to do this every year," Mum says. Now being in the financial position to make that happen is a great feeling. I smile and say "Definitely!"

⬡ Now it's your turn. Journal your destination (point B) now. Firstly list specific things or elements that will indicate you've successfully made your change. These things will likely be connected to elements you identified in your starting point. They will be tangible, measurable things that represent you have changed your circumstances around those things.

Next I want you to write what that new reality looks. Really have some fun with this and imagine how having made that change will unfold in your life. Go ahead and experience your change as if it's already happened. What does it feel like to have achieved this change? What does it look like? What are you saying to yourself? How has it impacted on your life to have made this change? Play full out and write about all the ways making this change has changed your life.

Why am I asking you to describe your new future so vividly? Remember how your brain does not know the difference between something real, imagined or anticipated when it springs into action to protect you. That very same ability can be used to assist create change and the life you desire. By imagining and emotionally embracing your future life now your brain begins to lock in new neural pathways that support that reality. Those pathways underlie new patterns and habits which assist manifest the change you desire. This may sound a bit farfetched but it's scientifically proven to be true. We look at this again later in the book. For now just consider the possibility and play with it.

Excellent! You've defined your destination and identified specific elements of it that allow you to measure change as it occurs. By imagining how that change will play out in your life you've also fired off new neural pathways in your brain to support your change.

Well done, your point 'B' has been established.

You have completed the first stage of the Change Made Easy process.

GET READY

"Reduce your plan to writing. The moment you complete this, you will have definitely given concrete form to the intangible desire."

– Napoleon Hill

Good Vibrations

> "Signs of a life that we cannot explain are everywhere, vibrating by the side of the life of every day.
> – Maurice Maeterlinck

At the start of this book I said it was going to expand your mind. Well, this may be one of those moments. Science now knows that solid things, including ourselves, are actually made up of more space than matter. Under a strong enough microscope atoms and subatomic particles are seen to have large areas of space between them. To give you an idea of just how much space we're talking about imagine the proton of an atom blown up to the size of an orange. Now place that orange in the middle of a football oval with nothing else on the field. That is how much space exists between the protons in the nucleus of a single atom.

Science also knows that atoms are not stationary. Everything in the universe is moving and vibrating. So next time you look at yourself in a mirror think about that. You are a form that appears solid but in fact are made up of mostly space that is vibrating. Each person has their own unique vibration that shifts and changes in response to many things. It may be referred to as their energy or the vibe they give off.

It is important to understand that everything is energy. That includes you and everything around you. The chair you sit on, the food you eat, the music you listen to, the very space that appears to be empty between you and the objects you look at. Vibrating energy, all of it. This may be a very new way for you to look at your world. Even the thoughts you have, the words you speak and emotions you feel have their own particular energy.

You are in fact an individual expression of energy existing in a sea of energy. While you have your own particular energy signature you are always vibrating and interacting with the sea of energy you're connected to. This sea of energy is known by various names depending on your field of study or perspective. Scientists may call it the quantum field. Others may call it the grid, the matrix or power of the universe. If your definition is faith based you may even call this omnipresent grid of energy God.

When you understand the underlying energetic nature of your own existence and your connection to an energy source much greater than yourself, you open to the possibility of cultivating that connection and putting it to work for you. That my dear reader is massive! You'll see how it all plays out at bit later.

Making Sense of It

> *"The reality of you lies much beyond your sensory perceptions and boundaries."*
> – Amit Ray

Let's talk about vibration. In very simple terms it's described as having a frequency depending on how fast it's vibrating. You use your senses to interact with and interpret the sea of vibrational energy you live in. Simply put, your eyes are the 'equipment' you use to interpret vibration visually. Your ears are the 'equipment' you use to interpret vibration as sound. Using our commonly known senses of sight, sound, taste, touch and smell we're able to interpret vibrations that fall within a particular range of frequencies.

There are many other frequencies all around us that our senses alone cannot pick up. That's because they operate on a frequency outside of the range of our senses. A dog whistle is a classic example of this. When you blow the whistle you don't hear anything. So why is it audible to the dog? That's because the frequency created by the whistle is within the range that is able to be heard by the dogs ear but outside the range of a human ear.

What about your radio? Talkback shows, songs, news and weather are being broadcast all the time. The frequencies are around you all the time, in that sea of vibrating energy you live in, but it's not until you turn on the radio and tune into the station of your choice that you're able to hear it.

The radio is the equipment that converts the frequencies into a form that can be interpreted by the human ear. It's the same with your TV. The appliance converts data into usable frequencies that can be seen and heard by your senses. Are you sensing just how busy this sea of energy, vibration and frequency is? It's just as well we're not able to pick up on all of it. To say it would overload us is an understatement.

While being bombarded with information is not desirable the ability to tune into extra information allows us to be more informed about changes we make. I believe at this time in our evolution our ability to perceive frequencies is expanding. Our 'frequency range' is growing rapidly and more and more people are able to pick up on things outside what is considered the normal range of our traditional five senses. This is known by some people as a sixth sense, others call it a gut feeling or intuition.

Thankfully the stigma and fear associated with an ability to tap into this is dissolving. It really is just the ability to pick up on a broader range of frequencies. As you learn to tune into and listen to information from this expanded frequency bandwidth you gain access to the intelligence of the sea of frequencies you live in. It makes perfect sense to use this intelligence in our decision making and approach to change.

I was aware of this sixth sense as a child (most children are) but was reluctant to explore or use it in my life as a legitimate resource until I was well into my adult years. As you may know, when something is meant to be it keeps being presented to you until you acknowledge it and learn what it has to teach you. I eventually 'got it' and for years now have been inviting and using extrasensory information in my personal and professional life. It is basically an expansion on the concept of everything as a vibrational frequency and being able to recognise and interpret that information.

Intuition and the ability to recognise extra sensory information has guided me and assisted me make many decisions and changes throughout my life and if you remain open to it, can do the same for you. Concepts that were once considered mystical now blend beautifully with cutting-edge science and can assist you make change. Learning to tap into and trust your intuition is just one more way to help you make informed decisions and consciously create the life you desire. .

Ripples

> *"Just as ripples spread out when a single pebble is dropped into the water, the actions of individuals can have far reaching affects."*
> **– Dalai Lama**

If you've ever seen a pebble dropped into water you will know the ripples it creates. You, as an energy source are just like the pebble. The energy that you generate radiates out past your physical body and ripples out into the sea of energy you are a part of. Each and every person is like a pebble or drop of water that falls into the sea of energy we are all a part of. This is how we are all connected.

Your energy is continually being broadcast into the sea of energy like a pulse. You generate your own energy which comes from within and extends out past your physical body, impacting not just you but others around you and the collective generally. Even without an understanding of this principle most people do pick up on this energy.

Have you ever walked into a room where people are watching TV, reading or going about their business? While nothing is obviously wrong you pick up that something is not right. The energy in the room is palpable. We've even got a phrase for it; "You could have cut the air with a knife." Later you find that people in the room had been arguing before you arrived. What you did here was intuitively pick up on the energy of the room. Energy is real. It is everywhere and the ability to read it and use it wisely is a skill well worth cultivating, for making change and for life in general.

This energy exchange is a two-way thing. As you send out your particular energy you are exposed to and impacted by the energy of others. Pulsing ripples are being sent out all the time that intersect, overlap and merge. So what determines the type of energy that your generate? The type of energy you generate is determined by your state. Merriam-Webster's dictionary defines state as: condition of mind or temperament. It's the particular condition of your mind or way you feel at any given time. You may also like to think of it as your mindset.

Your 'state' is fluid and will shift and change according to your circumstances. So what is it that causes you to feel a particular way? Here we come back to three key things that, if you haven't realised by now, play a major role in your perspective of life and your ability to successfully make change. They are your thoughts, words and emotions.

You are capable of choosing your state and able to move fluidly from one state to another. The ability to do this consciously is what separates us from the rest of the animal kingdom. Unfortunately the majority of people go about their lives with little or no awareness of the state they are in. This can cause all sorts of trouble with your attempts to make change. Becoming more aware of your state and creating a mindset that assists you make change underpins the Change Made Easy process.

The Magnet Effect

"Thought is a force – a manifestation of energy – having a magnet-like power of attraction."
– William Walker Atkinson

It's time to take a closer look at how the exchange of energy occurs between you and the sea of energy you live in. You operate as a receiver of energy as well as a transmitter. You also have the ability to direct the type of energy you generate, emit and attract back to you. The impact of this is massive! It is much more far-reaching than just picking up on the energy of the person next to you. It's the basis of how you manifest things in your life, including changes you wish to make. In just the same way that you control the energy you create, you are also in control of the energy you attract. In the simplest of terms, like attracts like. You are a magnet that attracts things to you that match the energy you emit.

A major reason people struggle with change is that they spend their time focused on what they don't want. They generate energy around that and send that energy out as a ripple into the sea of energy they live in. Under the law of attraction the collective field that holds all potentials identifies that energy and sends more of the same to them. They attract people, circumstance and opportunities that match the energy they sent out.

Remember, science knows that what you focus on increases. If you focus on what you don't want that is what you'll get more of. The change made easy process teaches you to shift your focus to what you want. This one simple thing will completely change the energy around your change. The principles are scientifically proven. All you need to do is apply the principles, allow them to work for you and become a magnet to attract what you want in your life rather those things you don't.

Reality TV

> "Your life experience is a moving picture, of which you are writer, director, performer, producer and critic."
>
> – T.F. Hodge

Reality TV is huge at the moment. People sit and watch the lives of others with intense curiosity. The Change Made Easy process encourages you to bring your attention back to yourself. Your focus is directed back to you, your life and the change you are making. Now knowing that you actually generate and attract the energy that creates your life puts you in a powerful position. When you understand you are the creator and director of your own life you ultimately see that you are the star of your own personal reality show. Your life is playing out before you like your own personal giant 3D movie.

The exciting part is that you are able write your own script. You are the star and other people in your life are bit players, characters you create to tell your life story. As the director of your life you determine how much impact other characters have in your story. You actually have the ability to write characters in and out or your script and decide if you are creating a comedy, drama or movie of another genre.

Now life would be pretty one-dimensional if all you did was watch one movie type. Life is certainly more creative than that and affords us opportunities to experience a range of things. Comedy, drama, tragedy, and romance are all a perfectly natural part of life. To have hopes and dreams and feel the highs and lows of our experiences and endeavours is what breathes life into our existence.

In the Change Made Easy process you develop an awareness of what channels your life has been running on. You come to understand that you have default channels you tend to watch. Ultimately you recognise that you have the ability to change channels. You are like a living breathing remote control, able to create a variety of life movies and vary your experience of life depending on what channel you select.

Each channel on the remote holds a different energy and will reflect a different perspective of life back to you. Your life is created and viewed through the lens of the energy you generate. Understanding your life as a reflection of the energy you are generating truly empowers you to make choices and choose channels to create whatever you want in your life.

Think about your life currently. What might the life movie you are currently starring in be called? It's quite possible to view different areas of your life on a different channels. Your professional life movie may be running on the action channel while your relationship movie may be running as a drama. Look at the list below and consider what channel you flick to when you engage in different parts of your life.

- Action
- Drama
- Angry
- Loving
- Grateful
- Happy
- Sad
- Abundant
- Healthy
- Unwell
- Anxious
- Comedy
- Successful
- Confident
- Afraid
- Mystery
- Adventure
- Romance

Awareness and choice are the key factors here. After identifying the channels each area currently operates on go back and consider if you would like to change any of those channels. If so, what channels would you prefer to be on? You have more channel options than Netflix, Stan and Foxtel all put together.

Your emotional state determines which channel you are on. These are not just your stock standard emotions such as love, anger, jealousy or joy. As the remote control of your own life you are much more advanced than that. You have channels for any feelings you can imagine. This includes things such as abundance or scarcity, courage or fear, wellness or dis-ease, being loved or judged. The list is almost endless.

So let's forget about getting lost in the drama of other people's lives. Turn the TV off and take time to look at your own life movie. The one you have created to date. Establishing that as a starting point and deciding where you want to go from there is when the fun begins. You begin the process of writing the script, the storyline and creating the characters of the life story you want to live.

You have all the required channels on your remote. As the star of your own movie you get to decide which channels you view your life on. What choices will you make for yourself moving forward? What might the life movie you are about to create for yourself be called?

Resistance

> "Resistance is thought transformed into feeling. Change
> the thought that creates the resistance, and there is no
> more resistance."
> – Robert Conklin

In this section of the book we're going to address some of those things that may have previously blocked you or caused you to struggle with change. Let's start by taking a look at resistance.

Resistance to change comes in all shapes and sizes. I used to amaze myself at just how creative I was at putting things off. There was no end to how resourceful I could be. Putting off getting on with something I knew I needed to do was a skill I'd honed over the years. I was a master procrastinator.

There was always some washing or ironing that needed doing. Some people have actually told me they find ironing relaxing, almost therapeutic. Let me assure you this is definitely not the case for me. I'd put ironing right up there with a trip to the dentist but even so, to avoid other things I've been known to make ironing a top priority. A phone call to a friend was another great distraction or catching up with someone for coffee. A quick look at what was on TV would often end up wasting hours of time. What about nipping down the street to do a bit of shopping? Perhaps I could combine shopping with catching up with friends and having a coffee all in one. That's a half day gone easily.

One of my all-time favourites was a time I sat knee deep in flat-pack furniture pieces trying to make sense of assembly instructions. It took me two entire days to put this furniture together and days more when you consider the time I'd spent shopping for and purchasing it. All that time spent on something that wasn't essential. What a brilliant way to distract me from more important things I had to do. Told you I was good at it!

Now, friends, coffee, TV and even washing and ironing all have their place. It's only when you use these things (or anything else that you use) to put off doing something that it becomes an issue. The trick is to become aware that you're doing it. With awareness you can make different choices.

The ability to step back and look at your life and the things you do without judgement can be very entertaining. Now if I catch myself looking longingly at furniture in catalogues or shop windows I laugh. Thinking back to my flat-pack episode I pause and consider if I'm actually doing it again. Am I just searching for some way to distract myself from things I have to do?

As you go about your change, become aware of the various ways you procrastinate. Are there things you do that merely distract you from getting on with making your change a reality? If you have recurring issues with procrastination there will be something underlying that, something that may very well be discovered and resolved as you work through this book. Because you are no longer judging yourself this becomes just another part of the intriguing journey you're on to understand yourself better.

It's not only you that may put up resistance to your change. Resistance can come from the least likely places. Often those closest to you, your family, friends and colleagues create resistance. Sometimes they will know exactly what they're doing. They'll have their own agenda and believe you making change is not in their best interest. The other possibility is that they are not consciously aware of what they're doing and would be mortified if they realised they were making things difficult for you.

What underlies any resistance by others is the fear that your change poses to them. At first glance there may be no obvious impact on them but any change that you make does ripple out and affect others. It goes to the connectedness of everything. For people closer to you, who know you in a particular capacity, the dynamic of that relationship will change with any change you make. Take a look at the following list. How many of these are you to other people?

- Mother
- Father
- Son
- Daughter
- Sister
- Brother
- Aunty
- Uncle
- Colleague
- Friend
- Lover
- Spouse
- Boss
- Employee
- Teacher
- Student
- Mentor
- Teammate

Any change that you make means your relationship with each of these people will shift. It could be very subtle or undeniably obvious. Regardless of how the relationship will be changed the fact that change is occurring causes an element of disquiet for them. Your change causes them to experience change also.

Remember what we spoke about at the start of the book. People are hardwired to resist change due to that part of the brain that springs into action in an attempt to keep them safe. If people around you feel threatened by the affect your change has on them, their brains get to work and create feelings, thoughts and behaviours in an attempt to protect them.

That can show up as something as obvious as a work colleague deliberately undermining your attempts at promotion. Whether they are jealous of your ability or in competition for the position the person involved knows all too well they're intentionally creating resistance or blocking you. That type of resistance is deliberate and, at first glance, made at a conscious level.

Other resistance is more subtle. What about the person who's focusing on health or losing weight. How often after declining food or drink not in keeping with their change do they hear, "Go on, one bit won't hurt you"? This is a resistance commonly offered by friends and family members. If you were to ask them they would say they fully supported your efforts in improved health and wellbeing. At a conscious level they are not even aware that their offers are in fact a source of resistance to your success and the change that will cause for them.

If you find this happening to you be gentle with those involved. Whether their behaviour is intentional or not, it all stems from fear. If they have not read this book they may not know where this fear comes from or even that it exists. Their behaviour may be completely unconscious. Perhaps you should lend them your copy of the book, or better still, gift them their very own copy so they get all the same benefits from this information that you are.

The Games We Play

> *"Creating success is a tug of war between your mind and your heart, your fears and your dreams."*
>
> – Robert G. Allen

Knowing you procrastinate is one thing. Understanding why and moving past it is a different ball game altogether. One of the most frustrating things when you make a change is feeling that you're fighting against yourself. It's not that you don't know what to do or how to go about it. To make matters worse it's as clear as the nose on your face that you're the one stopping you, sabotaging your efforts and not getting on with it. And make no mistake, you can have all the knowledge in the world, a spectacular plan and all the best support systems in place but unless you square this change away with **yourself** you will struggle with it or find a way to stop it occurring.

This section is about identifying and removing those blocks so it's time to pull up a couple of chairs and sit your subconscious and conscious mind down for a chat. You need to ensure that they resolve any conflict around your change and are on the same page. To make change easy you want both parts of your mind to hold hands and skip along this change path instead of playing tug-of-war with each other. When you do this it not only makes change must easier but also makes the process much more enjoyable.

Beliefs

> *"Man is made by his belief.*
> *As he believes, so he is."*
> – Bhagavad Gita

Your beliefs and values which are stored at the subconscious level are often a source of conflict between your conscious and subconscious mind. It is essential that these align with the change you say you want. You see, you don't get what you say you want – you get what you believe.

Let's take money as an example. You might say that you want ten million dollars. Sure, on the surface you can say what a wonderful difference that would make in your life. You can describe how you'd help others with it and what you'd spend it on. That all sounds great on the surface. But what if at the subconscious level you are running a belief pattern that people with a lot of money are pretentious snobs?

Perhaps you grew up hearing things like 'money doesn't grow on trees' or 'money is the root of all evil'. If you've heard of either of these two you may have a subconscious belief around money that it's hard to come by or alternatively you'll actually repel money as you want to be a nice person, you don't want to be evil.

These beliefs and values are powerful. Even if money does find its way to you, if your belief system does not support you having it, you will find a way for it to be gone. Studies have shown that up to 70% of people who've won multiple millions of dollars in lotto draws are broke again within five years. Whether it appears they squander that money on poor investments or lavish gifts for themselves or others the result is the same. By hook or by crook, situations and circumstances occur until they find themselves back in their familiar financial situation. They return to a financial state that aligns with their limiting subconscious beliefs around how money applies to them. Their mindset does not support that type of wealth.

Take a look at the list below and see if any of the statements are familiar to you.

- Money is the root of all evil.
- People with money think they're better than everybody else.
- We're not made of money.
- Money doesn't make you happy.
- It takes money to make money.
- We can't afford it.
- The rich get rich and the poor get poorer.
- What, do you think I'm made of money?
- Money doesn't grow on trees.
- If you have money others will go without.
- You're not good enough or smart enough to have a lot of money.
- The family has never been good with money.
- There is never enough money to go around.

At this time in your life you may not consciously believe these statements. Unfortunately even though you believe they're not true on a logical level, if you recognised any of them they may still exist in the

90–95% of your brain function which is happening on a subconscious level. They were likely imprinted on you years ago from family, friends or others around you. (Remember – no blame.) There's even a school of thought that beliefs can be handed down through generations via cell memory. What about reincarnation? Could your current beliefs be connected to a past life you have lived? That is a topic for another book entirely.

However you came to get these stored beliefs and values you took them on without your knowledge and with no awareness of how they were impacting your life. The very fact that you are now aware of them allows you to address this, get your conscious and subconscious mind on the same page and end the tug-of-war with yourself.

Planting Seeds

"Don't judge each day by the harvest you reap but by the seeds that you plant."

– Robert Louis Stevenson

People become very attached to their beliefs. Just try denouncing someone's political or religious beliefs and watch how passionately they defend them. But what is a belief really? A belief is a truth you create for yourself that requires no evidence. It is nothing more than an opinion you decide to hold true.

Just as easily as your existing beliefs slipped into your subconscious to create the way you see the world, with awareness you can now consciously change them. All you need to do that is to decide what your new belief will be and then tend to that belief as if it were a seed you've planted in your brain.

Remember that you have taken back control of your life and are now back in the driver's seat. Think of your brain as a garden and now decide what seeds you would consciously like to plant. Choose empowering belief seeds that support your change. Continuing on with the theme of money perhaps you might like some of these.

- I attract money easily.

- I am open to receive riches and abundance.

- There is plenty to go around.

- I am worthy of financial abundance.

- I am like a magnet that attracts success and riches.

- Money and prosperity flows to me day and night.

- I deserve and expect prosperity.

After you plant your seeds the next step is to tend them. The first way you do that is by giving them your focus. Science knows that what you focus on is where your energy goes. What you focus on grows.

To focus on something involves bringing it to mind. An awareness of your new belief seeds is the starting point. To tend your new beliefs you should check in on them regularly to maintain your focus on them. In time, as your new beliefs grow roots and take hold they will become more self-sufficient but in the early stages you need to nurture them just like a newborn. Remember the process of learning something new. It requires repeated exposure, consistency and repetition until it becomes your norm. This is exactly the same for your beliefs.

Your brain creates neural pathways to store information. This includes your beliefs and values. Those pathways become stronger the more they are used. Each time you use a particular path it is reinforced. Those old beliefs you've been running for years and years are well established, like a well formed hedge. To establish and strengthen the neural pathways of your new beliefs you need to redirect your focus and energy on them. As you do that and disengage from your old beliefs, the old beliefs are pruned away and their neural pathways weakened. The new beliefs take hold and become the new garden of your mind.

Now consider the change you are currently working on. This is your opportunity to complete the beliefs exercise in your workbook or your exercise book.

⬙ The first part of this exercise is to write down your current beliefs around the change you're making. Make a list of all those thoughts, opinions and beliefs you have that may have blocked you or caused you to struggle with your particular change.

It's an interesting exercise to pinpoint what may have been holding you back. Do you know when you took on those beliefs? It may be an opinion, belief or attitude you thought was someone else's but now realise it was 'gifted' to you and has been hiding in your subconscious due to exposure to it over the years. Without judgement, write a list of your current beliefs around your change.

Remember you can return to this list to add and adjust it at any time. The mind is a fascinating thing. When you ask it a question it continues to search for answers or information long after you've stopped focusing on it. Just like when you've forgotten someone's name or a movie title and out of the blue, perhaps a couple of hours or even days later, the name or movie title comes to you. Your mind had been dutifully searching for that information while you got on with life and were doing other things. Return to your workbook and update this or any other exercise should your mind offer up extra information at a later time.

Well done! You now have a list that gives you clues. You have identified beliefs that may be on the other end of that rope you've been pulling on.

While the first part of this exercise can be eye-opening and reflective the second part will energise you. Now you get to consider and choose new beliefs for this change. What beliefs would support you achieving your change? Remember, you need no proof of these beliefs. They are simply new empowering statements you're declaring as your new truths. Make them strong and bold. If it all feels like make believe, you are correct, as you do this you are actually making new beliefs.

You should now have two belief lists, your old list and your new empowering list that supports your change. Review both lists and ensure that any limiting belief on your first list has been negated with a strong, confident and bold belief in your second list.

Remember if it feels strange, that's a good thing. It feels that way because you are seeing things from a new perspective. It's different and that's exactly what it needs to be. You are in the process of changing your mind and that's exciting because when you change your mind, you change your life! If you feel resistance to this process at any stage I want you stop, step out of yourself and re-engage as one of the characters we introduced earlier. Play with it as a child would, explore it as an adventurer or become the scientist and see it as an experiment. Spend a little time in your neutral zone if you need to.

Excellent job! You've identified the opposition, those limiting beliefs that have caused you problems previously. You have also declared new empowering beliefs to assist you make your change. These are the seeds you have planted to create your new mind garden, a garden where change is embraced, enjoyed and made easily.

Values

> 'To feed what you value, to align your energy, attention, time and resources with what you say is important to you, starts to bring your power out of hiding."
> – Debrena Jackson Gandy

Another key thing to align your change with is your values. Your values are those things that are most important to you. Some values may be constant in all areas of your life such as honesty, integrity and compassion. Other values may be specific to particular areas of your life. In your work life you may value creativity, loyalty, and productivity. In your personal relationships you may value respect, humour and support.

I remember years ago when I first did a values exercise. It was when I studied NLP* and we were asked to make a list of what was really important to us in our lives. Initially the list is extensive and gradually you reduce it to the five things you value most in your life. I ended up with things like connection, joy, family, health and fun. It wasn't until after the exercise that I realised what I was currently working on in my own life was nowhere on the list. While I'd spent time adjusting my beliefs I'd been unaware that there was a conflict between my beliefs and my values. And I mean a massive conflict. When I reviewed my entire initial values list, my area of focus had not even made it onto the page.

*NLP stands for Neuro-Linguistic Programming – it is the science of how the brain stores and accesses information and how that forms our experience of the world.

Luckily for me, and you, values are fluid just like your beliefs. At any particular time in your life different values may rank differently on your list. And just like your beliefs, once you know what your current values are you are able to adjust them to support your change. Ultimately what you are looking to do is align both your beliefs and your values with the change you want to make.

✡ Now consider the change you're currently working on. This is your opportunity to complete the values exercise in your workbook or your exercise book. Do a general values list first. List all those things that are important to you generally in your life. There are no right or wrong answers. If you really value comic books or sleeping in late, write it down. This list is specific to you. Keep writing until you can't think of anything else then ask yourself again, what is really important in your life. Persist and come up with at least three more things. This list is likely to be quite long.

The next step is to review the list and pick your top ten. Then repeat it again and reduce it to five. Lastly you are going to prioritise your top five from one to five, one being the most important to you and working down.

When you do this exercise please don't try to cut corners and come up with your top five straight away. It's often much later in your list and even after you thought you were finished that values that are really important to you show up. Write your top five general life values down in order of importance. Great!

Now that you've got the hang of this, let's get specific. You are going to repeat the process you've just done but this time establish what your values are around the change you're making. Start a completely new list and ask yourself, in the context of this change, what is really important to you. Repeat the exercise you did for your general values but apply it to your change this time. After completing the exercise you will have a list of your current values around the change you are making, listed from one to five, in order of importance. Great job!

As you look at this list now consider if the values you have listed are values that support your change? Are there other values you should include in your list? In relation to the change you are making, what values would best support your success? If you struggle with this exercise, one way to select effective values is to consider what values someone else who has achieved a similar change would have used. You can model yourself on someone who is successful in the area you are making change. That includes using the values you believe they would have had to be successful.

Go ahead now and write the top five values, in order of importance that you believe will assist you make your change. This may contain completely different values than you had been using. It may be a mixture of old and new values. It may also involve rearranging the order of existing values you had on your list.

And there you have it. Values you can combine with your new beliefs to support, motivate and inspire you to succeed. The opposition has thrown in the towel. They have let go of the rope and come over to your side. You are now operating with a seriously strengthened team that is ready to work together rather than against each other. Excellent work!

Each time you use the Change Made Easy process make sure you check in on your beliefs and values and ensure they support you in the change you are making. They are like the skeleton that supports the life you create. We will flesh out your skeleton in the last section of the book. Congratulations on adding these two powerful players to your team!

Other Team Members

"Teamwork is the secret that makes common people achieve uncommon results."

— Ifeanyi Enoch Onuoha

As you continue to build a strong support team to assist you make change, who or what else do you think may assist you on your change journey? I touched on the science of epigenetics earlier. It explores the effect our environment has on our lives. This relates to making change also. Your environment affects your behaviours so to get better results when making change create an environment that favours you. Put yourself in environments that support you. That means that the people around you matter.

Businessman Jim Rohn said, "You're the average of the five people you spend most of your time with." While I agree with the essence of this message I think it is a bit limited. It's definitely worthwhile seeking out people who will inspire, encourage, and challenge you to make your change but that does not necessarily mean you need to leave other people in your life behind.

Some people in your life are invaluable just for their acceptance of you for who you are and their belief in you. They may not have any particular skills or knowledge that relate to your change. Regardless, to be loved and accepted unconditionally is priceless. As you learn to live a more authentic life you cultivate this quality yourself. Becoming more accepting of yourself you become more accepting of others and understand that each person is living their life their own particular way, not better or worse than yours, just different. Cherish your relationship with these people!

We've spoken about the various channels we choose to create and watch our personal life movie on. While we are able to and do change channels frequently there tends to be a default channel each person chooses to watch. I'm sure you know someone who always seems to be on the drama channel. Who do you know who operates on the angry channel most of the time? What about those who choose the success channel, the financially abundant channel, the fun channel or the romance channel? Think about the various people in your life now and see if you can identify their default channels. Whatever their channel is it's nothing more than a pattern they've locked in that has become the predominate way they create, view and experience their world.

The default channel that someone watches is often the way that others describe that person's character or personality. The way we develop our personality and how that affects our experience of life is captured in the following verse:

Be careful of your thoughts,
for your thoughts become your words.
Be careful of your words,
for your words become your actions.
Be careful of your actions,
for your actions become your habits.
Be careful of your habits,
for your habits become your character.
Be careful of your character,
for your character becomes your destiny.

– Author unknown

You did an internal stock take earlier to spring clean your values and beliefs so they support your change. A stock take of the people you spend time with is also a valuable exercise. It's not difficult to do. How do you feel when you spend time with someone? While everyone has good and not so good days, if someone regularly leaves you feeling drained and brings you down this does not support the positive optimistic approach to life that will assist you make change.

If you know people like this and they still have relevance in your life I would suggest you monitor the amount of time you spend with them. As you grow, evolve and make change it may be the role they play in your life has diminished. Accept that you have moved in a different direction and while honouring their life choices always make choices that support the life you are designing and creating for yourself. This may involve reducing the amount of time you spend with some people or in some instances, discontinuing the connection with them completely.

Some people you simply enjoy spending time with. They uplift you and are people you have fun with. It's nice to be able to just relax and have some down time from your change pursuit. These people are important as they bring a sense of balance to your life.

Your change 'A' team are those people who have knowledge, contacts or experience that specifically relate to your change. It may be someone who has already achieved what you're working on. Consider modelling your behaviour and actions on what they did. They are proof that what they did worked. They may also be a great mentor for you if they are open to taking on that role.

You want to spent time with people who push you and challenge you to make progress and achieve your change. These people may not have done the exact same thing you want to do but they bring something else to the table. It could be knowledge or technical skills. Perhaps they are the person who keeps you motivated, accountable and on track. Do they provide a service or program to support and encourage you? Take a moment to think of other types of people it would be good to surround yourself with to support your change journey. Who else would you like on your team?

Definitely never underestimate the importance of the company you keep. Support your aspirations, motivation and actions by placing yourself in environments that support you as often as possible.

Human nature is a funny thing. We are quick to blame our environment when things go poorly. If you lose a job, it was because of the downturn in the economy. If you lose a game, the referee was biased. Heavy traffic made you late for work. We find excuses without hesitation when things go wrong.

When we win, however, we ignore the environment completely. You got the job because of your talent and charm. You won because you were on fire and played an awesome game. You arrived on time because you were organised and prompt.

Remember that life is not happening to you, you are creating it with your every thought, word and action. Be mindful of where you spend your time and the people you spend it with. At all times be accountable for your progress your outcomes and your life and remember, the right mindset is crucial to successfully making change. As you move forward consider this:

> *"Whether you think you can, or you think you can't*
> *– you're right."*
> **– Henry Ford**

Let's Get Physical

"The moment you change your perception, is the moment you rewrite the chemistry of your body."
– Dr. Bruce Lipton

We have talked about creating the right mindset to assist you make change and also about those people and places you surround yourself with. Now let's take a look at how your physical body plays a part. You inhabit a body that is the most amazing self-regulating, self-healing creation known to man. You are a walking, talking, living breathing organic pharmacy.

Your body is constantly monitoring your internal environment and releasing chemicals and hormones in response to your state at any given time. The intelligence of your body responds to this like filling a script. Incredibly, Australians spend over $11 billion a year on medications. This inclination to seek external intervention to create a healthy internal state completely overlooks the fact that, given the right conditions, your body is often able to heal and create a balanced state on its own.

As a part of the Change Made Easy process you are developing a new level of awareness of how your thoughts, words and emotions affect your internal environment. That allows you to present different scripts to your body and encourage it operate in a balanced and healthy way naturally.

As you go about making your change do not overlook your basic physical needs such as sufficient sleep, good nutrition and plenty of water. Water makes up about 73% of the human brain. Remember that the brain is where you are planting the seeds of your new garden. It is the nursery of those new beliefs and values you chose to support you make change and move forward. As well as maintaining a focus on these new seeds, keep them hydrated to assist them take hold and become established.

Eat well, get sufficient good quality sleep and take time to get out of your head and move. These things all contribute to the environment you create for yourself. You know now just how important your environment is to successfully make change so support your physical body and allow it to support you in return.

Even your posture and facial expressions contribute to the script you ask your body to fill. There are some fascinating books around about body language. They interpret the way that different postures and gestures indicate how a person is thinking or feeling. This order of feeling to posture can be reversed and it's just as possible to intentionally manage your posture and gestures to support a particular way of thinking or feeling. Become aware of this and make it work for you. If you want to feel confident, stand tall, lift your head up and notice how your stance supports that feeling.

Knowing that your environment has such an impact on your life, let's look at one really simple thing you can do to create a positive environment. This one thing promotes wellness, enjoyment of life generally and also your experience of change. What is it? It's a smile.

The simple act of smiling sets off an incredible chain reaction in your body. This one action creates a cascade of feel-good hormones and neurotransmitters. A smile stimulates the reward or pleasure neurotransmitter, dopamine. Dopamine provides us with feelings of pleasure which causes us to repeat behaviours. This will come in handy when you take action towards achieving your change.

Dopamine has numerous other benefits including improved energy, focus, mood, attention, alertness and libido and provides feelings of joy, confidence, happiness, an overall sense of wellbeing and a mild euphoria.

Smiling also boosts serotonin. Serotonin plays a significant role in regulating body temperature, sleep, pain, mood, and appetite and improves self-esteem, our sense of wellbeing and contentedness with life as well. It is like a natural antidepressant and also produces mild euphoria.

Endorphins are another neurotransmitter stimulated by a smile. These neurotransmitters relieve pain, heighten self-esteem, and create feelings of wellbeing and a mild euphoria. Endorphins are known for their positive effects on mood after physical activity.

And to top this all off, because your brain is so amazing it will respond to a fake smile just the same as it does to a genuine one. So if you want to improve your overall experience of change, do it with a smile on your face. If you want to improve your overall experience of life, smile every day. I hope you can find something each day to genuinely smile about. If that's not the case in your life right now, and even if it is, do the following exercise to build the habit of smiling (and get all the associated benefits) in your life. You will be pleasantly surprised at the results. For all the parents out there, it's a great 'game' to play with your children. Definitely a game where everyone's a winner!

Exercise

- Put the largest smile you possibly can on your face and hold it there for a minimum of 30 seconds.

- Do this on three separate occasions each day.

- Do this exercise every day for one month.

That's it. Deceivingly simply isn't it? No special equipment required. No cost involved. No excuses! I know from experience that it works. I first did this exercise myself many years ago. I'll admit I felt somewhat silly doing it but stuck at it and now enjoy the benefits. Driving to and from work were my favourite times to do my smile exercise. I got the occasional strange look from other motorists or pedestrians but it was worth it.

I hadn't even realised I'd locked in the habit of smiling until friends and people at work randomly started asking me what I was smiling at. I was not even aware that I was smiling. The habit of smiling had become something I was doing automatically. Knowing all the benefits associated with that, it's a script I'm happy to get filled regularly by my internal pharmacy.

The Brains Trust

"Listen to the wind, it talks. Listen to the silence, it speaks. Listen to your heart, it knows."
– Native American proverb

Your change team continues to go from strength to strength. You have now recruited your body and mind and know how to use them to create an environment that supports you. Now let's look at how to access the wisdom of your brains trust to make the best choices and decisions about change. When we talk about the mind most people connect that back to the brain. Well, here's a bit of information that will blow your mind. They now say that we have more than one brain! That is why I use the term brains trust.

I'm not referring to the different sections of your head brain like the reptilian brain, the limbic system or neocortex. I'm talking about different organs in the body that appear to fit the definition of a brain. Part of that definition is to be capable of storing information and holding memory. Of course the brain we all know about does that, but research now suggests that our heart and our gut also operate as a brain. So it now appears that we have three brains that we know of currently and in time we may establish that other parts of our body are also by definition a brain.

There are certainly examples of people who have received a heart transplant who experience personality changes or have very different outlooks on life after the transplant. Sure, undergoing such a major experience would cause most people to re-evaluate and re-prioritise their lives, but there are stories that go far beyond that. Transplant patients have displayed characteristics and tendencies of the people whose heart they received. This is the brain-like quality of the heart in action as the memories contained in the heart play out in the person who received it. Fascinating stuff really. Here are a couple of examples of that.

Example 1

A 47-year-old white male foundry worker, who received the heart of a 17-year-old black male student, discovered after the operation that he had developed a fascination for classical music. He reasoned that since his donor would have preferred 'rap' music, his newfound love for classical music could not possibly have anything to do with his new heart. As it turned out, the donor actually loved classical music, and died 'hugging his violin case' on the way to his violin class.*

Example 2

An eight-year-old girl, who received the heart of a murdered ten-year-old girl, began having recurring vivid nightmares about the murder. Her mother arranged a consultation with a psychiatrist who after several sessions concluded that she was witnessing actual physical incidents. They decided to call the police who used the detailed descriptions of the murder (the time, the weapon, the place, the clothes he wore, what the little girl he killed had said to him) given by the little girl to find and convict the man in question *

*Pearsall, Paul. *The Heart's Code: Tapping the Wisdom and Power of Our Heart Energy.* New York; Broadway Books, 1999.

While it is very interesting to discover that different organs also act like brains, of what relevance is that to us in terms of making change? I believe that not only do these organs hold memory but also that different types of intelligence reside in these different brains in our bodies.

Let's look at those three brains now. Think about your head brain. This brain is like the library of the knowledge you have accumulated during this lifetime. It houses your logical, analytical and strategic brain as well as your creative, abstract feeling centres. We store learnt information here and reference it to make decisions on how we interpret and interact with our world. This is where the memories of this lifetime are stored that influence how we view the world and where we fit into it.

Next look to your heart. As a brain how do you think the intelligence stored here might vary from that in your head? The heart holds your intelligence at a soul level. It's the connection to the essence of you that inhabits your physical body. It is the connection to your Spirit. Knowledge at this level is very different. It knows the expansive, eternal you. When you tap into information from your heart you communicate with your higher self. It is the home where love, passion, purpose and connection to everything resides.

And lucky last, the gut. What's the intelligence of the gut? It's where your intuition lives. This is the ability to understand something instinctively, without the need for conscious reasoning or facts. We have sayings that point to this such as "I had a gut feeling" and "Trust your gut."

So we have these three sources of information to refer to when we consider change. Most people today live predominately in their head and make decisions from there. If those decisions are not aligned with what the heart and gut are trying to tell you it creates conflict. That conflict may relate to you choice of change, how you experience the change and how successful you are at achieving it.

Part of the Change Made Easy process is to tune into information from all three brains. Leaning to listen to information from you head, heart and gut gives you information on multiple levels. From there you can make the best decisions, decisions that are in line with your true purpose. This consultation process resolves conflict between the brains and clears the way for you to move on with the change.

In line with living authentically I suggest you filter any change you intend to make through your heart. Remember this is the point that connects you back to your Spirit. It's that part of you that knows it's connected to everything and will always make decisions from a place of love. That is love for yourself and others. This is definitely a habit worth locking in. It's simple to do yet will change the way you approach your life.

Here is a very simple exercise to drop into your heart so you can filter your thoughts, feelings and ideas around change, or anything else for that matter. This can be done anywhere and requires no special equipment. It is centred on your breath.

While it's nice to sit comfortably and remove distractions to do this, it can be done anywhere. That may be sitting at your work desk, travelling to or from work, at the dinner table while the kids are driving you crazy or waiting in the queue at the supermarket… you get the idea.

Heart Filter Exercise

Just become aware of your breath. The very moment you do that you take your attention off of external things going on around you. Your focus is directed to your chest area, the area of the heart. If it is safe for you to do so, close your eyes. This also reduces your focus on external things.

Breathe in through your nose and out through your mouth. Become aware of the air as you breathe in. Notice how it travels down deep into the base of your lungs and feel how the lungs and ribcage expand on the in-breath and relax again as you exhale through your mouth like a long easy sigh. Find your own comfortable rhythm, slowing breathing in and out.

And now, as you continue breathing in and out, simply allow your focus to shift slightly and connect specifically to your heart. There are many ways to know you've connected with your heart. You may get a sense of warmth and softening in your chest. You may feel your heart expanding and opening, like a flower or the lens of a camera. Perhaps it creates an incredible sense of calm. However

---

your heart speaks to you, you will know when you have connected with it.

Now consider any thought, emotion or idea you want to filter through your heart. As you breathe in, just allow that to be drawn down with the breath into the chest and heart area. Some things move quickly and slip straight down into the heart while others may take a bit longer. Simply continue to focus on your breathe and allow it to make its way there.

You will sense when it arrives. My personal experience is that what I'm filtering diffuses and blends with the energy of my heart. What's your experience? Just breathe and notice. After considering your thought, emotion or idea, draw your focus back to the connection with your heart. Sit with it for a few breaths and then tune into any information you get now about your original query. Know that the information you receive now has been filtered through the heart and has the benefit of the wisdom of your higher-self.

As you move forward, to assist you make change easy, tune into and listen to all the information available to you. That is the logic, knowledge and creativity of your head brain, the intuition from your gut brain and insights from your higher self which are accessed through your heart. This is the way to make heart-felt change and live a heart-centred life. Use the combined wisdom of your brains trust to assist you make decisions around change.

Plot your Course

> *"Goals are pure fantasy unless you have a specific plan to achieve them."*
> – Stephen Covey

Now that you've established your starting point and your destination we are going to plot your course. You have assembled a strong team to support you as you move forward and identified and removed those things that previously stood in your way. I would just like to take a moment to congratulate you on your progress so far. Did you know that a large percentage of people who buy books don't ever read them or never actually finish them? Whether you are choosing to do the exercises along the way or are content to just read the information at this stage, you are showing up and doing it. Pat yourself on the back and know that by reading this book you are already taking action towards achieving your goals.

Now, let's create specific steps to move from your point A to your point B. First things first. When you plan out your steps it's important they are well-spaced. Have you ever taken a hike and encountered steps that were spaced at awkward intervals or heights. This can turn a planned day's walk into a real chore rather than the invigorating, enjoyable trek you'd imagined.

The same principle applies to the journey you're taking with your change. As you plan your steps space them so you can enjoy the journey. That is not permission to stay in your comfort zone. It's absolutely necessary that your steps stretch you. If they don't do that you will just mark time and get nowhere. Make sure that the steps you take actually move you forward.

As you plan your steps never underestimate what you're capable of. You should also know that pushing too hard can be detrimental to your progress. Just as well-spaced steps will stretch you, poorly-spaced steps may break you. The Change Made Easy process contains a review stage to ensure this does not happen to you. As with all parts of the Change Made Easy process you can and should review your progress as you go. If you need to tweak your action plan and steps you can so relax and enjoy outlining the path you intend to take to make your chosen change.

How many steps does your change involve? It will depend on the change you're making and your flexibility. Just how much can you stretch? Remember there is no right or wrong way to go about this. This is your change and it's perfectly OK that you go about making it your way. Letting go of the opinions of others about how or at what pace you make change is liberating. As you stand in your own truth you become more aware and accepting of the unique person that you are. You understand that your steps will be specific to you, just as your change and indeed your life is specific to you.

Break it Down

> *'The man who removes a mountain begins by carrying away small stones.'*
> **– Chinese proverb**

I will use the earlier example of wanting change around financial circumstances. Often people get stuck and don't make change as they become overwhelmed with where to start and what to do. The way to move past this is to break the situation down into smaller pieces. Originally I listed four specific elements around current financial circumstances. They were credit card debit, trouble servicing car payments, a mortgage that saw no money left over to enjoy life and a personal loan outstanding to parents. That is the very first breakdown right there. From there each one can be further broken down, from man-size, to snack-size and ultimately to bite-size so you can get stuck into it and successfully achieve the change.

If I continue to use that example the steps may include doing or exploring the following things:

Credit Card

- Shop for deals to transfer balance at favourable introductory interest rates.

- Arrange for manageable regular payments to be made direct from salary to credit card.

- Cease use of card till the balance is paid off.

Car

- Contact car finance company to negotiate a way forward.
- Sell the car and ride a bike or use public transport.

Mortgage

- Contact loan provider to discuss different, more manageable repayment options.
- Engage a broker to search for possible options to refinance the loan.
- Get financial advice regarding living arrangements such as
  - Selling the house and renting.
  - Selling and purchasing in a different location.
  - Downsizing to a smaller house.
  - Taking in a boarder to supplement income.
  - Renting the house out and living in a less expensive rental property.

Loan to Parents

- Regular manageable direct payments made from salary until loan paid back.
- Flowers and card to say thank you for their generosity, support, love and patience.

There would be another list to address general things regarding finances including things such as;

- Reduce general spending by
  - Making lunch instead of buying lunch each day.
  - Be more energy efficient around the house (turning lights off in rooms not in use, setting heating levels slightly lower etc.)
  - Curb general spending on non-essential items.

- Get professional advice re budgeting.

- Consider a debit consolidation program.

- Become more educated in money management.

You see how the original list can expand quite quickly. The above list is by no means exhaustive and I'm sure you could think of ways to break it down even further. Lists can contain layer upon layer upon layer.

After breaking down your change into bite-size chunks the sheer number of lists can seem overwhelming. The way around that should it occur is simple. Just deal with one list at a time. In the above example you may initially choose to focus on just your credit card. Once you've achieved that specific element you can move onto your next financial element. And so it goes as you gradually adjust and change your relationship with managing money.

Bit by bit you establish new patterns and habits that eventually result in you achieving your original goal which was an improved financial position. By focusing and taking action on the little chunks the big picture takes care of itself. When you plan your steps out this way your experience of change will be much more manageable, enjoyable and achievable. Eventually you will look back and realise just how far you have come.

⭐ Now it's your turn. This is your opportunity to complete the 'plot your course' exercise in your workbook or your exercise book. You have your starting point and end point so go ahead now and construct your steps. Start with one element of your change and break it down. List individual steps that will be required to achieve it. Remember to make your steps manageable. You want to enjoy this trek you're taking. It should invigorate and stretch you but not break you. Break down each element and keep breaking it down until you have lists of bite size chunks. Bon appetite!

Congratulations! You have assembled your team and outlined the path you will take to bring about your change. You are primed and ready to go.

You have completed stage two of the Change Made Easy process.

GET ON WITH IT

"The journey of a thousand miles begins with one step."

– Lao Tzu

Ready to Roll

> *"You don't have to be great to start but you have to start to be great."*
> – Oprah Winfrey

So here we are. You've done the groundwork, laid a great foundation and are perfectly positioned to successfully make your change. While the principles in this book are universal the way people take action it is a very personal thing. You may find each time you apply this three-step process you tweak it slightly. That's perfectly normal and actually important. Life is not a one size fits all. Just work the process and allow the process to work for you.

From the behind the scenes work you've done so far you are now approaching your change with a new level of awareness. From this new perspective you're able look to at change, and in fact yourself, differently. You have effectively upgraded your brain by encountering the information in this book and completing the exercises along the way.

Let's review just how far you've come. The dot points below are like a pre-flight checklist. As you read through them if any are unfamiliar, go back and re-read that section of the book. After all, I want you to have a smooth enjoyable trip as you proceed with your change.

So far you have:

- Reviewed you current circumstances and acknowledged your currently reality. You know your starting point.

- Clearly identified the change you are making and what it looks like to achieve it.

- Considered if your change is authentic and enhances your own unique expression of life.

- Created a neutral zone where you go to dissolve and release any negative judgement towards yourself and others in relation to your life and the change you are making.

- Selected a character to assist you approach and experience change from a new, novel perspective.

- Understood that any feelings of apprehension towards change and new things are completely normal and hardwired in your brain as a protection and survival mechanism. (Your misguided friend.)

- Viewed change with a new perspective that transmutes fearful, depleting energy to anticipation and energy to propel you forward.

- Learnt your brain is capable of producing a complete experience from thought alone. It does not care if the situation is real, imaginary, current or not.

- Discovered that where your focus goes, energy flows. What you focus on grows.

- Become aware you are a source of energy that acts as a magnet and draws to you the same type of energy that you emit.

- Realised it is just as easy to direct your thoughts to create an experience you want rather than one you don't.

- Aligned your beliefs and values with the change you want so your conscious and unconscious mind work together and assist you rather than play tug of war.

- Mapped out a plan to take you from A (your current reality) to B (your desired change).

- Designed a plan that breaks the change down into achievable action steps.

- Acknowledged that highs, lows and hiccups are all part of making change and it is your response to this that matters.

- Discovered the importance of spending as much time as possible in environments that support your change.

Congratulations on playing, exploring and experimenting with the concepts covered so far. And while everything you've done so far has prepared you perfectly, all the planning in the world won't create something unless you engage with those plans and take action. So buckle up, here we go, let's do this.

Action

> "Knowing is not enough; we must apply.
> Willing is not enough; we must do."
> – Johann Wolfgang von Goethe

Now that you are aware just how important your mind is in this change process it should come as no surprise that starting out each day in the right state is vital. Time spent selecting the channels you intend to view your life movie on is like getting dressed for the day. Just as you consider what outfit to wear, what energy do you want to create, radiate and attract as you go about your day? You are in control. You get to choose. Each morning you have the opportunity to create your mindset. Make this your first action step and harness and direct the power of your mind to move forward with a sense of excitement and purpose to achieve the change you want.

Personally, each morning I give thanks for the new day. Yes, even when the alarm clock goes off at some ungodly hour of the morning with it still freezing and pitch dark outside. Admittedly I often bemoan the fact I have to leave the warmth and security of the doona but I soon snap out of it and feel immensely grateful for my life. After all, I've just spent the night in a warm bed, safe and secure. There are others who do not have that privilege. The alarm clock and my good friend the snooze button get me up to go to a job I enjoy that financially supports me. Again, many people are not so fortunate. Reminding myself of just how lucky I am, each morning I stretch and greet the day by giving thanks and saying the following mantra that expresses my own personal outlook on life.

"Good morning world! Thank you, thank you, thank you – for another day and opportunity to play, learn, grow and contribute."

By all means feel free to use it or take a moment to think of one of your own. Being in a state of gratitude and having a sense of opportunity is a wonderful way to approach each day.

Place Your Order

> *"You must ask for what you really want.*
> *Don't go back to sleep."*
> – Rumi

The next step is to turn your attention to the specific change you are working on. Focus on that change now. Think of this like sitting in the restaurant of life and looking at the menu. There are endless options and you get to choose what it is that you'd like.

You may be focusing on a specific, tangible thing or directing your focus on a more generalised way to experience your day. Personally, when I first started this practice I focused on my mental state and the overall way I engaged with my world. I would select three or four emotions or states to bring into my day. Some of my favourites were (and still are) joy, abundance, connection and gratitude.

Alternatively you may have a tangible, specific goal or thing that you want to change or bring about. It may relate to improved health, relationships, your career or finances.

So go ahead and place your order now. See the change you want in detail. See it completed and just look at the end result. Take a bit of time here to really paint the picture of having successfully made this change. You may like to refer back

to the exercise earlier in the book where you identified the change you would work on. Flesh it out now with all the details you can imagine.

If you find yourself slipping into old habits or thoughts such as you are not worthy or what will others think of you; just notice that. Acknowledge it and thank it for having been a part of your life, then simply let it go. It's either that old friend (the hardwired part of your brain concerned with survival) misguidedly attempting to protect you or just remnants of old thought patterns, based on old beliefs that had probably been with you a long time.

As you recognise these thoughts and feelings for what they are any negative energy associated with them shifts. Apprehension dissolves and energy previously trapped in negativity transmutes into energy available to help you make your change. Instead of being drained of energy at the thought of change you become charged with energy.

Sure, you may still have butterflies. You may still feel unsure. Any time you expand your experience of the world and do something differently, this is natural. You are stepping into your unknown. The big difference is in your awareness and understanding of this. Rather than creating negative, debilitating energy based on fear you are now able to harness that energy as anticipation and excitement to assist you make the change.

It's time to get the team together. Earlier in the book you established new beliefs that are part of and support your new future. These are new truths you have chosen for yourself. I want you to tap into those new supporting beliefs now. Say them to yourself or better still, say them out aloud. If you need to refer back to the earlier beliefs exercise to re-establish your connection to them that's fine.

And now it is time to do the same for the values you chose to assist you with your change. Review those top five values now, connect with them and say them out aloud.

Once you have fully engaged with your new beliefs and values move back into your neutral zone and know that you are now working with your new, upgraded mind. If it feels like you are making all of this up, that's fine. Just play with it, experiment and see where it takes you.

Do not concern yourself with how your intended change will come about at this stage. Understand that this order you are placing is independent of your current circumstances. Your current reality is of no consequence as it is a product of your **past** beliefs, focus and actions. The Change Made Easy process involves altering these things and aligning them with the future you want. Doing that actually begins the process of creating that future for yourself.

I can't help but smile and get excited as I write this. It's one of my favourite times of the day. To use the power of my mind to create my day (and my future). This level of awareness puts you back in control of your life and in a position to create your life by design rather than default. How good does that feel? Let's find out.

Feel It

> *"Feelings are much like waves, we can't stop them from coming but we can decide which ones to surf."*
>
> — Jonatan Mårtensson

Once you have clearly defined your change (placed your order) it's time to cook it and allow it to come to you. This is the step that prepares your order and brings it from the universal kitchen right to your table to enjoy.

This process has a magical quality to it. It seems incredible that we have the power to collapse ideas and thought into physical reality but it is true. Let's look at it from a very practical viewpoint. Everything that man has ever created started initially as a thought or idea. Take shoes as an example. We were not born with them. They don't grow on trees but at some stage someone got sick of cold feet or sharp rocks and decided to do something about it. The first version was likely a piece of animal hide left over from a kill to feed the tribe. Someone thought to wrap a piece of hide around the foot to protect it. Over time, other people had ideas and thoughts on how to improve that initial foot covering until here we are today with an entire industry around shoes for every possible occasion. And still it continues to evolve as designers and fashionistas come up with new ideas and concepts for how we cover our feet. It all starts with a thought.

Now let's look at the power of partnering a thought with a supporting belief. It was in 1954 that runner, Roger Bannister, first broke the four-minute mile in a time of 3:59.4. Prior to that it was generally believed that the human body was not capable of achieving a four-minute mile. As part of his training, Roger repeatedly visualised the achievement in order to create a sense of certainty in his mind and body that it was possible. Actually achieving it created the belief in others that it was possible and since then many male athletes have achieved sub four-minute mile times.

So let's apply this powerful partnership principle to your change. Having defined your focus, stand in your neutral zone where you are free from any limitations or negativity. Now become childlike. Believe in magic and that anything is possible – that **your desired change is possible**. This is the powerful state that prepares you to achieve what you want.

And now it's time to animate your change. This is like pressing the button on your energy remote control and setting the energy frequency you operate on. It is an essential part of the process and creates your energetic environment. You know that you resonate energy out into the universe that the universe picks up on and responds to. Dr Joe Dispenza describes it something like this. He said that if the thought sends the order out, the emotion or feelings attached to it is what collapses the thought from the quantum field back into your physical reality. Thought sends it out – emotion draws it back. Both parts are required. It's like posting the order for your desired change into the quantum field and attaching a self-addressed envelope for it to be delivered back to you.

So how do you animate your change? You do this by embodying the thing you are focusing on, completely, with all of your senses, as though **it is already your reality**. We touched on this earlier in the book and now it's important you understand the significance of it and embrace it. Remember that the brain is capable of creating a full body experience, regardless of if the scenario is real or imagined. With this awareness we are now going to use that to our advantage.

Let's have a practice run. You need to be specific and identify what particular energy you want. For the point of the exercise let's work with the energy of confidence. Regardless of what change you are working on this is energy will assist you achieve it. Confidence supports your belief you can successfully make change. It will also assist you move past any reluctance or discomfort connected to doing new things. It is a powerful energy that can be used in any area of your life.

So you have the word. You can see it on the remote. Now you need to push the button to move to the channel of confidence and generate that energy. The way you push the button is by fully embodying the word. That involves using all your senses to experience confidence.

Do that now. Recall a time when you were completely confident. You were unstoppable and knew beyond any doubt that you were totally capable and able to achieve what you wanted. Perhaps it was a work or social situation or sporting event. It may be something that you do every day with complete confidence. It need not be a big event. The example you use may have happened recently or many years ago.

If you struggle to recall a personal example of supreme confidence you can use an example of someone else. This may be a real person or even a superhero from a movie. You can model any example of someone who is supremely confident for the purposes of the exercise.

Now as you think about this time when you, or the person you are modelling, felt supremely confident become very clear and aware of the experience:

- What does confidence look like to you?

- What does confidence sound like to you?

- What does confidence feel like to you?

- Are you saying anything to yourself when you embrace confidence?

Immerse yourself in the experience of confidence. Animate it until the word expands into sensations that fill your entire body. When you feel this shift you have tuned into and pressed the confidence button on your remote and are now generating the energy of confidence. Well done!

The simple process you have just done can be used to access any form of energy you want. It works by choosing a specific type of energy

then recalling an example of an event when you felt that energy. The key factor is to embrace the feelings until they flood your system. At that point that you have pushed the remote button and are generating that energy.

So now let's select the remote channels for your chosen change. Focus on your change now. That thing you have defined in detail. It's time to animate it by feeling what it feels like to already have it. What does that look like? Is this a tangible thing? If it is, touch it now. Feel the texture and shape of it. What colour is it? Is it big or small, light or heavy? Can you taste it? Does it have a scent? Does your change put you in a particular environment? Are you outside? Can you feel the sun on your face or a breeze against your skin? Are there sounds associated with your change? Are you saying something to yourself or can you hear other people perhaps applauding or congratulating you on your success in whatever you have done or changed? Go for it! Play full out with this so that your imagined future can collapse from thought into form and show up in your physical reality. This is how you flesh out the skeleton of your beliefs and values.

Remember, do not concern yourself with how that will happen. Just let your imagination run wild and **see your change fulfilled** with all that means to you.

As you do this exercise understand that the universe is extremely literal. The more specific you are in describing the change you desire the more detailed order you are placing. The most important thing of all is that as you do this exercise you imagine it, embrace it and feel it as though **it has already happened**. Flood your body with the emotions of it **already being your reality**.

If you imagine your future in terms of wishing it to be the case the universe will deliver you circumstances and situations that will keep you in a state of wishing it were so. To be effective, you must **see, imagine and feel it as though it is done**. Placing your order with that energy signature compels the universe to respond in like. While it feels like magic it is actually based on scientific principles.

Well done! You have just taken the first practical step to getting on with it and making change easy. It really is that simple (and fun) to take a few minutes each morning to actively and with awareness, create your day. Abracadabra! Like magic you evoke the universe to get on with the job of collapsing aligned quantum energy from thought to matter to form and deliver your order to you. The energy signature of having successfully made your change now radiates out around you and into the world of quantum potential. Having placed your order with the universal kitchen go about your day knowing that your order is being prepared.

Day by Day

> *"Give every day the chance to become the most beautiful of your life."*
> – Mark Twain

Your job now is to go about your day with an awareness and expectation that your change is on its way to you. The exercise you just completed created your change or future on an energetic level. Having done that you should not annoy the chef. Leave the preparation of your order to the universal kitchen and get on with your day.

As you go about your day be aware of people, opportunities and circumstances that show up. Ask yourself, could they possibly be a part of your order being delivered back to you? Be open to the many varied ways that may happen. Maintain a focus on your desired outcome but do not place limits on how that will occur. The universe can and often does come up with opportunities, solutions and pathways you had never imagined for yourself. All you need do is be open to that, recognise when such things are presented to you and take action.

And action really is the name of the game. Motivated, purposeful, enjoyable action. So while you keep an eye out for unplanned opportunities from the universe it is time to refer to the action plan you constructed earlier and get on with that.

What does it mean to take action? It means to engage with your change, as the word suggests to act and do something. Ordering, visualising and emotionally embracing your change at the start of each day is the first step. This sets your remote control to radiate energy in line with the change you are focusing on. That exercise is universal and allows you to use your imagination and tailor it specifically to each change you make. After that the type of action you take will depend on the particular change you are working on. Individual action plans may consist of a series of different steps, a particular step or action you need to repeat over and over or a combination of these things.

To instil new habits and behaviours requires repetition. Remember the four stages of learning until something is running at an unconscious level. This means that to effectively change a pattern of behaviour, to lock in a new way of doing something until it happens without conscious thought, you normally need to do it over and over again. How many times? It varies considerably.

A common myth was that it takes 21 days to change a habit. That started in 1960 when a Dr Maltz, published his findings that patients took on average 21 days to identify with their changes after undergoing surgery. We now know better. Later studies have shown that while some changes can happen and 'stick' in an instant, it more commonly takes a couple of months and sometimes much longer.

As a Master NLP Practitioner I have seen people make instant change and release old ingrained beliefs and patterns in one session. It is remarkable to witness just how pliable the human mind is. In scientific and medical circles this is known as brain plasticity or neuroplasticity. I've also seen it take time to gradually replace old patterns of behaviour and lock in effective lasting change.

My own personal experience of change is varied which I think is common to most people. While I make some changes at the drop of a hat at other times I'm like the horse that baulks at the jump. When that happens, guess what I do? I apply the very same process you're learning in this book. I check if the change I'm considering is in my best interest. I take a closer look at what I want and why I want it. Then I check in on my beliefs and values around my change in case they need to be tweaked. Remember unless your values and beliefs are aligned with what you say you want you will just play tug-of-war with yourself and make the change difficult if not impossible. After identifying the steps required to make the change I ensure those steps are broken down into achievable bite-size chunks. Finally I gather my team around me by surrounding myself with supportive people and seek outside assistance when required.

The Change Made Easy process really is a strategy for life. You can return to it any time you find yourself struggling or feeling stuck. It works on many levels to improve your overall experience of where you are at, where you want go and how it is you get there.

Do not be deterred by the fact that it may take some time to achieve your change. There is a reason that this book is called 'Change Made Easy' and not 'Change Made Quickly'. Take heart in the fact that the background work you have done has prepared you to have a completely different experience of change. That is my wish for you. To embrace change, enjoy the process and achieve results.

> *"Direction is so much more important than speed.*
> *Many are going nowhere fast."*
> — Unknown Author

Set a pace that's right for you. Do not to put yourself under the pump and feel pressured to achieve every change at lightning speed. Where's the fun in that? Setting unrealistic targets for yourself just sets you up to fail. Do that often enough and you will actually develop a pattern for failure. Even if you do stick with a hectic unrealistic pace the stress you put yourself under would surely sap any enjoyment from the process.

What we are all about here is making change easier. You do that by having the right mindset, setting appropriate benchmarks, and taking inspired action towards your goals.

As you plan and implement each individual change never lose sight of the bigger picture. Every change you make and goal you achieve is ultimately just another stepping stone on your life path. As you lay each stone and create your path always remember to enjoy the process, take your time and enjoy the view. Life is meant to be lived, not rushed. It is as much about the journey you take as it is about where you end up.

"When you dance, your purpose is not to get to a certain place on the floor. It's to enjoy each step along the way."

– Wayne Dyer

Consistency

> *"The secret of success is consistency of purpose."*
> – Benjamin Disraeli

So we've established that a level of commitment is required to make change a reality. Just how often and how much time do you dedicate to your change? This will vary dependent on the particular change you're working on and your circumstances. Regardless of what your change is or how much time you're going to allocate to it, a key ingredient in achieving change is consistency. My old music teacher, Mr Robinson, knew that and told me many years ago it was better to practise for 30 minutes each day than to practice for three hours once a week. Regular, frequent exposure or involvement with something produces the best results.

Because it's easy to get side-tracked with all that life throws at us let's look at a few things that can help you be consistent. Here are a few strategies to help you take regular action and get that change to stick.

Piggyback. A great way to help you lock in a new habit is to attach it to something else you already do on a daily basis. The existing behaviour acts as a cue for the change you're installing. Let's look at a couple of examples.

Example 1

As an aid to improve your general health you decide to drink more water. To do this you would first need to know how much water you currently consume each day so you can increase your intake. Unless you do this you will not know if you've been successful in making a change or just redistributing when and where you drink the same amount of water.

For now let's assume you've not been a big water enthusiast and the change you want to make is to include water in your diet every day. This could be as simple as deciding to have one glass of water before meals. If you eat breakfast, lunch and dinner and follow this strategy you will add three glasses of water to your daily intake. Simple but effective.

Example 2

Staying with the health theme, let's assume you want to incorporate some physical exercise into your day. Again, you can choose a particular time of day or context to introduce change. I will use bedtime as an example. Committing to something as basic as ten sit-ups each night before getting into bed may be your starting point. Don't like sit-ups, knock yourself out, make it ten star jumps, push-ups or whatever takes your fancy. Make it a requirement before you can actually lay down. The cue here is bedtime. While the actual time you go to bed may vary from day to day the trigger is constant. Each time you go to go to bed you are reminded to take action and do your exercise.

Consistency is the hallmark of new habits. Even with something as simple as the above examples you will initially still need to focus on it. Over time what once required your focus and attention becomes automatic. When that occurs you know you've successfully installed your change or habit. Consider if the above principle could be applied to or adapted to your change. What existing behaviour do you have you could use to piggyback the introduction of a new behaviour?

Buddy up. Pair up with someone, get a buddy or join a group to support you in your change. It could be someone who wants to make the same change you do. You can motivate each other and share in the journey. It may be someone who cheers you on from the sidelines and supports you make your change. Another option is joining a support group or an industry group specific to the change you are making.

Could you adapt any of the following examples to your change?

Example 3

For your general wellbeing you decide you want to take a walk each day during your lunch break. You invite people to join you and three colleagues accept your invitation. You now have companions to share the experience with.

By sharing your plans for change with others you get it out of your head and formally make the declaration it is something you intend to do. Remember the process of creation – from thought, to matter, to form. By voicing your intentions you have started that process. Your fellow walkers now also assist to motivate you and hold you accountable.

Example 4

You want to be more comfortable speaking in public. Enrolling in a class or group that specifically supports your change such as Toastmasters may assist. Having formally scheduled classes is another way to build consistency into your action steps.

Example 5

You have a phobia that impacts your life and prevents you doing something that's important to you. Sourcing someone with the expertise to assist you creates a knowledgeable support base and scheduling appointments promotes consistent action.

Time allocation. Most people today are very busy. Not having enough time is right up there as one of the most popular reasons people say they cannot make change. I know all about time constraints. In the past I had a long commute to a corporate job and worked twelve-hour shifts.

The 'time' excuse used to be one of my personal favourites. In reality, even with my long work days, there were plenty of opportunities to take action towards making change. Where might this time have be hiding in my day? Depending on the action steps to be taken I could have used breaks at work or the time spent travelling to and from work. My down time (watching TV) could have been reduced or coupled with one of my action steps. Who knew it was possible to watch TV while moving rather than sitting still? Most people are able to find some time hidden in their schedules if they really want to look.

> *"The key is not to prioritise what's on your schedule but to schedule your priorities."*
> – Stephen Covey

Allocating specific blocks of time in your weekly schedule to dedicate to your action steps (regardless of what they are) demonstrates your commitment to consistently take action to achieve your change. Schedule it in your diary or use the template in your workbook. You are effectively making an appointment with yourself to engage with your change. It's important that you treat this appointment with as much respect as you would for any other important appointment. Should other nonessential events crop up or people place demands on your time you must not defer to them and allow them to encroach on time allocated to your change.

If you are one of those people who till now thought nothing of breaking an appointment with yourself and put everyone else first ask yourself this. Could this be a beliefs issue? Do you believe that other people are more important or worthy of your time than you are? Perhaps you believe they will judge you if you don't accommodate their request. What about this one. Is doing things for other people a very sneaky way of procrastinating? On the surface you think you are needed elsewhere and others could not possibly do without you but really you use these requests to put off taking action towards your change. These are all things to consider if you find yourself breaking those appointments with yourself. Now that you are able to step back and look at these things without judgement studying your own behaviour can be fascinating.

The Change Made Easy process is effective when all of its elements are combined. Just like the elements of a great cake, if you leave out some of the ingredients the result will not be the same. Be consistent with all parts of the process. It is equally important to apply the universal exercises consistently as it is to take consistent action steps specific to each change.

Start each day by ordering your desired change, as specifically as possible, from the Universal menu. For the chef to cook it up you must embrace your change emotionally, as though it is already your reality. This effectively presses the energy channels that you are operating on for your day.

Check in with these channels periodically throughout the day to make sure you have not slipped back onto an old default channel. Often your reaction to a situation or person will point that out to you. If that happens, which is not uncommon when you first start out, just take a moment, embrace the feeling of the energy channel you want and reset yourself. Each time you make an adjustment like this you strengthen the neurological pathways associated with the energy you want and your old default channels are weakened.

Refer to your new beliefs and values often. They also need attention to become established. Perhaps you can piggyback checking on these at the same time as you check your energy channels. As we will cover next, motivation is what moves you to action. Remind yourself why you want this change regularly to fuel your enthusiasm.

This is your opportunity to schedule specific time to dedicate to your change. Ultimately some time should be set aside each day to maintain your momentum. Do the consistency exercise now in your workbook or exercise book to commit to the change you are making.

I will let you in on a little secret, consistency is a forgiving master. Life happens and there may be the odd occasion when you miss your action steps. While consistency is always the aim, the occasionally missed opportunity does not significantly impact on the habit forming process. If this happens do not use it as an excuse to give up. Think of your desired change as an election. Elections are won by tallying up all the votes. If you occasionally register a vote that does not favour your change (don't take planned action) it will not affect the entire outcome of the campaign.

Motivation

> *"People often say that motivation doesn't last. Well, neither does bathing – that's why we recommend it daily."*
>
> **– Zig Ziglar**

Motivation is an interesting concept. What is it that inspires us to shift from the familiar? And after we embark on change what is it that motivates us to persist and lock in new habits that achieve lasting results? It is said that if your 'why' is big enough nothing will stop you. Your motivation comes not so much from the end result you are after but why you desire to get there.

Think about that in relation to your chosen change. We touched on it earlier when we spoke about making authentic choices. Now I want you to look a bit deeper. What is your underlying reason for wanting to make the particular change you are working on? These reasons are what fuel your motivation. If something is really not that important to you, at the first sign of any hiccup you are likely to stop because it really doesn't matter to you that much anyway. On the other hand, if you have compelling reasons you will keep going regardless of hiccups, hurdles or hardships.

There are a number of things that move people to change. Often it is what is known as a pain point. Things get to a point where they are too painful to endure and change is made to move away from that pain. This is what is known as 'away from motivation'. While this can be a very effective way to get started, once someone moves sufficiently away from the pain to where it is bearable or gone, that original motivation ceases to exist. This can result in sliding back into old patterns of behaviour until the pain point is reached again. This potentially creates a yo-yo type cycle that is repeated over and over. The focus of this type of motivation is where you have come from, or what you are wanting to get away from.

Another type of motivation is 'towards motivation'. As it suggests this is when someone is motivated by wanting to move towards something. Towards motivation clearly identifies what you want, the reasons you want it, and keeps your focus on moving forward.

Both types of motivation are effective. In a lot of instances a goal will contain a combination of away from and towards motivation. Some people just work better with one type of motivation than the other as they have a stronger connection to it. You may start out using away from motivation and then switch to towards motivation as you make progress.

Now that you understand that everything is energy I want you to look at your source of motivation from that point. Towards motivation is more energetically friendly and enduring. You know now that what you focus on grows. When you use away from motivation you engage with energy that is in some shape of form unpleasant for you. If it wasn't you would not want to move away from it. This is fine in the short term but not ideally where you should spend all your time. Just as you now know to apportion the amount of time you spend with negative people, be aware of how much of your motivation stems from a negative viewpoint.

People are also motivated intrinsically or extrinsically. Intrinsic motivation is when you are motivated by an internal desire because you enjoy the behaviour in and of itself. The behaviour itself is its own reward and you require no external acknowledgement or benefit from it. Extrinsic motivation is based on external results. This could be receiving recognition for a job well done, a positive gain or avoiding a negative outcome.

When you go about making change motivation is important, hugely important. It is the thing that moves you to action. When you establish just what it is that motivates you, put those reasons in front of you at every given opportunity. Write them out and stick them on the fridge. Get an old lipstick or marker and write in on the bathroom mirror. Write them on the office whiteboard. Make them your screen saver. If there are appropriate affirmation cards stick them up somewhere you will see them often. Have some fun with this and make your own cards that remind you why you are doing this.

Why should you do this? Motivation is not a static thing. You will be more motivated at some times than others. Interestingly, sometimes, if your focus becomes fixed on the end result, motivation levels can actually drop. Reminding yourself of just why you are making a particular change will help you remain motivated. Your why needs to be right in front of your face and at the top of your mind for you to keep moving forward. As we touched on earlier, if you develop a habit of remaining focused and motivated to take just the next step, eventually the big picture will take care of itself.

Complete the motivation exercise now in your workbook or exercise book. Write down all the reasons why you want to make your chosen change. Spend some time thinking about what motivates you both extrinsically and intrinsically. Consider if your reasons are away from or towards based motivations. If more than 50% of your reasons are based on away from motivation, look at ways to switch some of those into towards motivation statements. This will have you focusing more of your energy on forward momentum, towards what you want. There are no right and wrong answers to this exercise. What is important is that you find your WHY and let that be what moves you to action on a daily basis. Go for it!

Celebrate Success

*"The more you celebrate life,
the more there is in life to celebrate."*
– Oprah Winfrey

While it seems like an obvious thing to do, you may be surprised. We are very good at beating ourselves up when we don't achieve something but slow to acknowledge our success. Perhaps that's a product of belonging to a nation well known for not letting people get too big for their boots. For the tall poppy syndrome where people are wished well and rooted for as the underdog only to be knocked down if they do too well. It's generally considered poor form for someone to blow their own horn and big-note themselves, regardless of how successful they are. Well, this is a book about change and it's definitely time to change that. Change Made Easy advocates recognising, acknowledging and celebrating your progress and success.

This is not about inflating egos and grandstanding, it is about genuinely acknowledging when you take action, move towards and reach milestones and goals. This may be a simple moment of pause and metaphoric pat on your back or rewarding yourself in some way for the achievement. Some of my personal favourites are time-out to watch a good movie, a catch up with a friend for coffee or even an extra hour sleep-in to recharge and be ready for my next step. Perhaps it involves sharing your progress and success with others who support you along the way. The reason to celebrate is twofold.

Firstly, you deserve it. You've taken time to consciously consider the changes you are making and taken steps towards your goal. You have chosen to create your life by design rather than default. By now you know that while the mechanics of making change are easy, the application of those mechanics still require work. You are doing the work and deserve to celebrate your progress.

Secondly you may have heard the phrase that success breeds success. Well it's true. When you succeed at something your body releases neurotransmitters such as dopamine that produce a sense of pleasure and motivation. It feels good and you want more. The brain does not care if you measure success in baby steps or giant strides. It responds to achievement the same way for both. That's great news to those of us who prefer to move forward gradually.

Your job, as part of the Change Made Easy process is to have identifiable checkpoints and milestones built into your action plan. These are points that indicate you have made progress and are moving in the right direction. They are points you undertake to pause and celebrate your progress. Like viewing platforms where you pause briefly to take in the view and look back along your path to appreciate how far you have come. How often you do that is up to you. Celebrate each and every step you take if you like or pick points along your action plan to acknowledge your progress. Perhaps you would prefer to acknowledge each day you take action or reward yourself at the end of each week for your efforts. However you do this it is important that you formalise the process.

This is an actual part of the Change Made Easy process and I want you to think about different ways you will celebrate your progress. Don't skimp here. What type of things would you enjoy as a reward for your progress and achievement? This needn't cost much. You may like to pour yourself a bubble bath and spend time having a good soak. Spoil yourself with a massage, pedicure or manicure or indulge in a good movie. Get creative. Choreograph your very own celebration move and cut loose, just like the player who makes the winning touchdown at the super bowl. Perhaps you can enjoy applying the change you have made in your life in some specific way.

Remember that this celebration is not a luxury, it's an important part of the process. Rewarding your progress not only fuels your motivation but also adds to your enjoyment of the change process.

⭐ This is your opportunity to complete the rewards exercise in your workbook or exercise book. Create a list of things you could do to celebrate your progress, both along the way and on achieving the change you are working on.

Make yourself a menu of rewards. It's important that this is not just a wish list. The list must contain actual things that it's possible for you to do. It represent things you can and will implement to celebrate your success as you achieve it. You can either allocate particular rewards to your chosen milestones now or if you prefer, refer to your menu each time you reach a milestone and select whichever one appeals at that particular time. As with all parts of this process, your rewards menu can be reviewed and amended at any time.

Review

"If plan A doesn't work, the alphabet still has 25 letters."
— Claire Cook

While the Change Made Easy process contains specific stages and requires you to commit to an action plan please know that those plans can be changed at any time. In fact it is important that your original plans are reviewed regularly to make sure they are still appropriate and serve the change you say you want.

At any time you may change your mind about the change you are making. You may change the actual change you want to make. Changes may be required to your action plan. The steps you planned will shift and change as you move along your path. You may decide to space your steps differently or discover and add new steps to your plan. Your mind may offer up new information or ideas that will change your motivation or even your beliefs and values around what you are working on. All of this is fine. Remember that change is natural and occurring all the time. That also applies to your change plans.

By taking time to review your plan and progress you will identify what is working and what you should adjust. If you find you have stalled you can return to those key elements of the process to determine what is holding you back. Is there a sneaky limiting belief that still needs to be replaced? Perhaps there are more powerful values that will assist you complete your change. Do you need to tend your newly planted seeds more often so they can develop, grow and become the new garden of your mind? And what about your environment. Are you putting yourself in environments that support your success? Do you have the right team around you? That includes the people you spend time with and where you spend your time.

If all these things are in place and your progress stalls it's time to consider your motivation. Review why you wanted to make this change in the first place. Do you have compelling reasons for wanting this? If you have honestly changed your mind then it's OK to let it go. Life is too short to pursue things and spend time on things you don't really want. Having said that if it is something that you really want take the advice of Winston Churchill and never, never, never give up.

Some of the 'under the bonnet' things covered in the Change Made Easy formula can take time to lock in. The concepts may be new to you, not only regarding change but about the very nature of your life. The seeds you have planted may need more time to become established. Perhaps your ability to select and remain operating on energy channels that support you is still developing. Do not underestimate these concepts.

They are like the magic sauce that goes over the basic mechanics of making change, filling in the gaps and joining the entire process together. Once you master this process your experience of change will be forever altered.

⭐ This is your opportunity to allocate time to review your change plan and progress in your time schedule. Do that now in your workbook or exercise book. Review your plan and your progress at least once a week.

Congratulations, you have completed the third stage of the Change Made Easy process..

It's a Wrap

> *"In the end she became more than she expected.*
> *She became the journey and like all journeys, she did not*
> *end, she just simply changed directions and kept going."*
>
> **– R. M. Drake**

Well, you did it. You have completed the three stages involved in the Change Made Easy process. I told you we were going beyond the mechanics of making change and that we have. There is a lot of information sprinkled throughout the process that makes it different from any other. Whether you realise it or not at this stage you have taken on board empowering concepts to assist you move forward and embrace change from a completely new perspective.

Because we did cover so much you may find it useful to return and re-read parts of the book at your leisure. As the process of learning is assisted by repetition, this will help you to lock in the information at a deeper level. Consider the book a companion for life that you can return to at any time to assist you make change. While having this information on an intellectual level is nice, there is no substitute for experience. Apply it, explore it and notice how your experience of change is altered.

At the start of the book I explained that the concepts would be covered in a simple way. If you would like to explore these concepts further there are a number of different texts listed in the suggested reading section to get you started. I have also included a checklist of the elements of the Change Made Easy process as a quick reference guide.

It has been my absolute pleasure to bring this information to you. The Change Made East process changes lives. If you would like to share your experience of it I would love to hear from you. You can do that at Changemadeeasybook.com. The site also offers other resources to assist and support you create a life that you love. If I can help you in any other way it would be an honour to join you on your journey and be part of your change team.

Enjoy your journey, wherever it may take you. Be inspired to create a life that celebrates the unique person you are. Amaze yourself with the power you have to do that and create and live a heart centred life that you love.

Now, in keeping with the process you have just learnt, I think this is a perfect time for you to celebrate and acknowledge your progress. Take a moment to reflect on the potential of the information you have just taken on-board and what that means for you and your life. Then refer to your rewards menu and treat yourself – you deserve it.

Change Made Easy
– Quick Reference Guide

- Select a change.

- Create your neutral zone.

- Establish your starting point (A) and identify why you want to make this change.

- Define your destination (B) and identify how you will know when you have made it.

- Plan bite-size steps to move from point A to point B.

- Be mindful of any resistance.

- Check that your beliefs and values support this change.

- Create and put yourself in environments that support this change.

- Find your 'why' – what is it that motivates you to want to make this change? Put your why in front of you at every given opportunity – it is what moves you to action.

- Set your energy each morning to align with the change you are making.

- Be aware of people, circumstances and opportunities that present during your day as potential connections to your order.

- Make appointments with yourself to formally allocate time to spend on your change.

- Take action daily from your action plan.

- Filter thoughts, ideas and questions about your change through your heart.

- Smile!

- Visit the nursery regularly. Set times during the day to check in on your new beliefs, values and selected energy channels. Reset them as required.

- Create a rewards menu and celebrate your progress and achieving your change.

- Review your progress at least once a week to check what is working and what needs adjusting.

- Focus on the steps and the goal will take care of itself.

- It is OK to make changes to your change plan.

- Enjoy the process!

About the Author

Karen Wilson is an author, speaker, facilitator and intuitive healer.

Enjoying the big-smoke in small doses, Karen is a country girl at heart. One of five children, Karen grew up on the Mornington Peninsula with a love of animals and passion for sports and music.

Later working in emergency services, for years Karen was a first responder and witnessed first-hand how people struggled with crisis and trauma in their lives. Whether due to circumstances or their outlook, so many people were unhappy.

With a strong desire to see people celebrate and enjoy their lives Karen spent many years studying the human condition from a number of different perspectives. The body, mind, spirit connection is emphasised in the multidisciplinary approach to the work she now does. As a facilitator Karen teaches people how to take control of their lives and discover and use the power they have to create what they want.

With a philosophy that true health and happiness are found in living an authentic, heart-centred life, Karen is dedicated to educating and inspiring others to fully embrace and enjoy their lives.

Author of the book *Change Made Easy*, Karen lives in Central Victoria, Australia.

Recommended Reading

This reading list contains a diverse range of subjects. It contains a sample of some of my favourites from over the years.

- Chopra, Deepak; *SynchroDestiny*. Random House 2003

- Hawkins David R. MD, PhD; *Power vs. Force*. Hay House 1995

- Dyer, Dr Wayne; *Living an Inspired Life*. Hay House 2006

- Gerber, Richard MD; *Vibrational Medicine*. Bear and Company 2001

- Schnabel, Rik; *The Power of Beliefs*. Brolga Publishing Pty Ltd. 2013

- Tolle, Eckhart; *The Power of Now*. Hodder Headline Australia Pty Ltd. 2000

- Jeffers Susan; *Feel the Fear and Do it Anyway*. Random House 2007

- Dispenza Dr Joe; *Breaking the Habit of Being Yourself*. Hay House 2012

- Dispenza Dr Joe; *You are the Placebo*. Hay House 2014

- Pearl, Dr Eric; *The Reconnection*. Hay House 2001

- Pearl, Dr Eric and Frederick Ponzlov; *Solomon Speaks*. Hay House 2013

- Carroll, Lee; *Lifting the Veil: Kyron Book 11*. The Kyron Writings Inc. 2007

- Redfield, James; *The Celestine Prophecy*. Bantam 1994

- Emoto, Masaru; *The Secret Life of Water*. Simon and Schuster UK Ltd. 2006

- Choquette, Sonia; *The Power of Your Spirit*. Hay House 2011

- Lipton, Bruce H. PhD; *The Biology of Belief*. Mountain of Love/ Elite Books 2005

- Millman, Dan; *The Way of the Peaceful Warrior*. New World Library 2000

- The Dali Lama and Cutler, Howard MD; *The Art of Happiness*. Riverhead Books 2009

- Canfield Jack; *How to Get from Where You Are to Where you Want to Be*. Harper Collins 2007

- Braden, Gregg; *The Divine Matrix*. Hay House 2007

- Zukav, Gary; *Soul to Soul*. Free Press 2007

- Hay, Louise; *Heart Thoughts*. Hay House 2012

RECOMMENDED RESOURCES

Do you want a dynamic speaker and trainer to present to your group, club, school or workplace?

Karen Wilson is an inspiring speaker renown for motivating and empowering others to achieve their best.

In a fun and informative environment participants achieve more confidence, self-awareness, resilience and sense of connection. Engagements create the potential for massive change in the lives of attendees and in the day-to-day operations of groups they belong to.

PRESENTATION FORMATS

Keynote

This engaging presentation will leave your participants energized and excited about the information they have just learned.

Please allow 1 – 2 hours

Full Day or Half Day Workshops

These programs are tailored to suit the outcomes and objectives of your organisation. Using exercises, activities and group experiences, these workshops achieve awareness and personal growth and provide practical strategies to build resilience among participants. This not only develops personal wellbeing but enhances team effectiveness and workplace morale.

www.ingramcontent.com/pod-product-compliance
Lightning Source LLC
Chambersburg PA
CBHW061045110426
42740CB00049B/2184